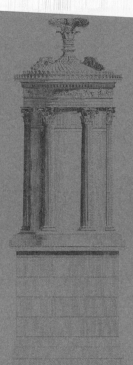

Léon Krier
(2003 Laureate)

Demetri Porphyrios
(2004 Laureate)

Quinlan Terry
(2005 Laureate)

Allan Greenberg
(2006 Laureate)

Jaquelin Robertson
(2007 Laureate)

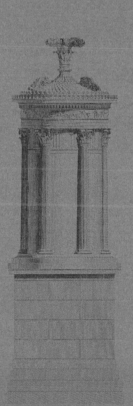

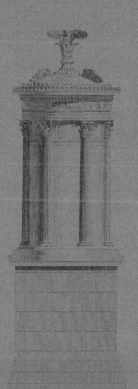

Andrés Duany
Elizabeth Plater-Zyberk
(2008 Laureates)

Abdel-Wahed
El-Wakil
(2009 Laureate)

Rafael Manzano
Martos
(2010 Laureate)

Robert A. M. Stern
(2011 Laureate)

Michael Graves
(2012 Laureate)

TIMELESS
ARCHITECTURE

TIMELESS
ARCHITECTURE

A Decade of the Richard H. Driehaus Prize at the University of Notre Dame

Foreword by Paul Goldberger

THE UNIVERSITY OF NOTRE DAME SCHOOL OF ARCHITECTURE is grateful to Richard H. Driehaus for making the Richard H. Driehaus Prize at the University of Notre Dame possible. Thank you as well to Matthew Walsh and the other members of the University of Notre Dame School of Architecture Advisory Council; Rev. John I. Jenkins, C.S.C., Thomas G. Burish, John Affleck-Graves, and the other officers of the University of Notre Dame; and to those who have served on the Driehaus Prize jury Thomas Beeby, Adele Chatfield-Taylor, Robert Davis, Elizabeth Meredith Dowling, Anne Fairfax, Thomas Fisher, Paul Goldberger, Léon Krier, Elizabeth Plater-Zyberk, Jaquelin Robertson, Witold Rybczynski, David M. Schwarz, and David Watkin.

First published in Great Britain in 2013 by Papadakis Publisher

 PAPADAKIS

An imprint of New Architecture Group Limited

Kimber Studio, Winterbourne, Berkshire, RG20 8AN, UK
info@papadakis.net | www.papadakis.net

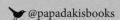 @papadakisbooks   PapadakisPublisher

University of Notre Dame School of Architecture
110 Bond Hall, Notre Dame, IN 46556
www.driehausprize.org | www.architecture.nd.edu

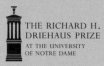
THE RICHARD H.
DRIEHAUS PRIZE
AT THE UNIVERSITY
OF NOTRE DAME

Publishing Director: Alexandra Papadakis
Design Director: Aldo Sampieri
Production: Juliana Kassianos
Editor: Kara Kelly
Editorial Assistance: Sheila de Vallée
Consultant: Lucien Steil

ISBN 978 1 906506 30 8

Cover Illustration:
A Classical Perspective; The First Decade of the Driehaus Prize
Carl Laubin
165cm x 250cm, oil on canvas, 2012

Frontis
A Classical Perspective; The First Decade of the Driehaus Prize, working drawing Carl Laubin

TABLE OF
CONTENTS

THE RICHARD H.
DRIEHAUS PRIZE

"Beauty, harmony, and context are hallmarks of classical architecture, thus fostering communities, enhancing the quality of our shared environment, and developing sustainable solutions through traditional materials."

–Richard H. Driehaus

The Richard H. Driehaus Prize at the University of Notre Dame complements the classical and urbanist curriculum of the School of Architecture, providing a forum for celebrating and advancing the principles of the traditional city with an emphasis on sustainability.

Established in 2003, the Richard H. Driehaus Prize is awarded to a living architect whose work embodies excellence at the highest level in traditional and classical architecture and urbanism and creates a positive cultural, environmental, and artistic impact. In conjunction with the Richard H. Driehaus, the School presents the Henry Hope Reed Award to recognize achievement in the promotion and preservation of the principles of the traditional city, its architecture, and art. Together, the $200,000 Driehaus Prize and the $50,000 Reed Award represent the most significant recognition for Classicism and tradition in the contemporary built environment.

The Driehaus Prize and Reed Award honor conservation and investment, a creative process that connects the past, present, and future, and celebrate architecture of sustainability in the best sense of the word. They set the examples and demonstrate the depth of commitment that we expect from our faculty and hope to instill in our students.

–Michael Lykoudis

Francis and Kathleen Rooney Dean,
University of Notre Dame School of Architecture

PAUL
GOLDBERGER

Foreword

The essays in this book are published in celebration of the first decade of the Driehaus Prize, the international architecture prize given in recognition of the ongoing strength and relevance of traditional architecture in our time. The ten writers are the first ten winners of the Prize, which confers on its recipients a bronze model of the Choregic Monument of Lysikrates, one of the iconic structures of Classicism, along with $200,000, making it the most valuable architecture prize in the world as well as one of the most prestigious.

It is no surprise that all of the winners express gratitude to Richard Driehaus, the founder of the Prize, and that some of them express astonishment that their commitment to traditional architecture, which for so long has seemed to exist at the margins of architectural practice, would be honored so generously. But the real value of these essays is not the appreciation of the Prize that they demonstrate, but something far more important that they reveal about how the best of the architects who choose to build in a traditional manner in the twenty-first century think—in other words, the way that these essays explain why these architects do what they do.

It is common, certainly among modernist architects, to view architects who design in a traditional manner as if they were Luddites, ideologues who are dead set against the present, and who deal with their objections to contemporary architecture by denying the reality of their own time. The Driehaus Prize winners, or at least most of them, do nothing of the kind. What is striking about the writers of these essays is how fully they seem engaged with the present, not mired in the past. The winners of the Driehaus Prize for the most part do not view themselves as crusaders trying to turn the clock back by pursuing a holy war against the modernist heathens, but as architects who understand and accept the broad sweep of history, and take pleasure in the multitude of architectural voices. They are comfortable with pluralism. What they are inclined to reject is not all of Modernism, but Modernism's own rejection of history. They have rejected the rejection, so to speak, and sought to position architecture once again as a "great continuum," to use Louis Kahn's phrase as Jacquelin Robertson did in his essay.

The Driehaus winners generally avoid the absolutist stance, the fundamentalist view, which turns architectural debate into a rhetorical fight across an unbridgeable chasm rather than a meaningful and productive dialogue between parties who, whatever their differences, share basic beliefs. Allan Greenberg described his own preferences thus: "In New York, where I now spend most of my time, I marvel at the genius of Rockefeller Center, the city's noblest urban space; and the Empire State Building, which will always be tallest because it is the very best skyscraper ever built…. And I ask you, are these two works of architecture classical or modern? I don't think it matters. They are both classical and modern; and they are both masterpieces."

Greenberg went on: "We should base our architecture on ideas more profound than the current oppositions of classical and modern, of tradition and innovation. That debate is about style and opinion. If we are going to have divisions, let them be about matters of substance, like freedom and tyranny."

Léon Krier is not noted for his sympathetic view of Modernism—he finds it, almost without exception, unforgiving and cold—but he states that "the brutality of Modernism is at its most extreme when and where it reigns supreme," and he notes that "Not by chance did Modernism produce its best results when it was a minority exercise in the 1920s." Krier then makes the unusual and generous observation that "The renewed competition is now improving the products of both recent Modernism and Classicism"—a comment that implicitly accepts the pluralism of our time.

Robert Stern, for his part, expresses the hope that "the day will soon come when tradition can be reconciled with modernity, leading to a cessation of the twentieth century's civil war between the two, replacing it with a more nuanced approach that puts human values over ideology and dogma." Stern continues: "In hoping for this foolish waste of artistic energy to play to a conclusion, I am encouraged by the words of the great Finnish architect Alvar Aalto, who was frequently asked, 'Are you traditional or modern?' To which Aalto would always and wisely reply: 'There are only two things in art: humanity and not.'" Today more than ever architects must be traditional and modern.

Creativity, the Driehaus winners tell us, is what matters, and they are united in believing that Classicism, when properly understood, is less a literal prescription than a set of rules and guidelines that can encourage truly inventive design. Indeed, there can be danger in treating classical principles too rigidly: "in teaching the Orders today we should take care that students do not become overly dependent on bookish authority," write Andrés Duany and Elizabeth Plater-Zyberk. "They must not learn the fear of being caught 'incorrect.'"

Classicism, then, is not dogma but wisdom handed down from our elders: that is the key message that these essays offer us. It is wisdom that we can choose to learn from or not, and that each will learn from it in his or her own way. But we ignore it at our peril.

"There is always a precedent. Nobody actually created anything new out of nothing," says Demetri Porphyrios. "Nobody created anything new or invented anything out of a vacuum. So the classical is the precedent. We look at that as a background, as a precedent against which we create something new. And that is that ability of the classical to encourage the production and the invention of the new."

The making of the new is the point, with traditional architecture as much as it is with modern. That is the lesson that these essays seek to convey, as it is the lesson of the Driehaus Prize itself. All architecture owes something to what has come before it. Classicism, used properly, does not have to constrict us or keep us in the past. In the pages that follow, all of the Driehaus Prize winners show us, with eloquence and passion, ways in which classical architecture can also hold forth the possibility of a richer, deeper and more satisfying present, enabling creativity of the highest order.

RICHARD H.
DRIEHAUS

Classicism is Local—and Global

In its first decade, the Richard H. Driehaus Prize at the University of Notre Dame has honored laureates from France, Great Britain, Spain, Egypt, and throughout the United States. In a world becoming too blandly homogenous, the Driehaus Prize-winning architects have sustained a vibrant sense of place through their commitment to Classicism in all its forms.

The Roman architect Vitruvius addressed the ethos of architecture, declaring that quality depends on social relevance. What creates social relevance in Santa Fe will not do the same in Saudi Arabia, but classical architecture's underlying spirit shines through aesthetic differences in buildings that give voice to their unique local contexts.

Beauty, harmony, and context are hallmarks of classical architecture, strengthening communities, enhancing the quality of our shared environment, and developing sustainable solutions through the use of traditional materials. These timeless ideals have endured for centuries, but now they have become even more essential as a means of preserving our cultural heritage, protecting our economic and environmental resources, and restoring a sense of continuity and identity that bonds communities.

Architecture shapes how we think about our sense of place. Sustainable by definition, classical architecture and traditional urban design facilitate the ways people live, work, and worship together. A dozen of the world's most iconic buildings, placed side by side, would not speak to each other. They might work separately, but not as a whole, not as a community. Modern architecture's vain elevation of individual expression over contextual necessities creates that sort of social dissonance. Classical architecture and traditional urban design foster harmony.

Although modern buildings might look futuristic in a science-fiction sort of way, classical architecture represents the best investment in the future. The modern vision for what architecture should be has become too shortsighted. The immediate interests of developers, the incentives of tax laws, and the narcissism of starchitects are causing economic and environmental waste. A good design doesn't cost, it pays over time—in the social capital of a strong community, in the savings of energy and material costs of buildings that can endure for centuries, and in the preservation of our increasingly finite natural resources.

At once respecting and improving our built and natural environments, the work of the Driehaus Prize laureates inspires delight. They design buildings with soul, a spirit that grows from recognizing that we occupy a place on a continuum from the past to the future. The footprint we make in our time must not trample our inherited influences, nor reduce the sense of possibility for generations to come. In an array of cultural contexts, I'm proud to say that the architects the Driehaus Prize has honored all exemplify sensitivity to past and future alike, while displaying inspiring originality in contemporary work that will endure. Their buildings will endure not only because of their beauty, or the quality of their design and construction, but because their attention to local context enriches the built environment. These are buildings that future generations will fight to preserve because they represent their cultures, their neighborhoods, their families.

The Driehaus Prize provides a forum for discussing these principles, for affirming the preeminent place of the traditional city and its architecture, and for restoring Classicism to the essential role it must play in building a sustainable future. We see embodied in the work of our laureates the essential truths of Classicism, the reasons why it has endured. They carry our best traditions forward. And through the Driehaus Prize, we will continue to honor the importance of that work and its power to shape our lives for the better.

MICHAEL
LYKOUDIS

A Larger View of the World

The mission of the Richard H. Driehaus Prize at the University of Notre Dame is twofold. On one hand it seeks to provide a forum for the discussion about the principles of the traditional city and its architecture; on the other hand it strives to reposition in the public mind the role that Classicism and tradition play in our future. Through the work of its laureates the Driehaus Prize has come to represent a larger view of the world—one that accepts the many dimensions of our modern world and links them within a framework that makes their interrelationship legible. This view is one of optimism and hope that we can reconcile the critical issues of our time and keep those values and objects that have made life meaningful and wonderful for millennia.

Classicism is the idealization and representation of nature with respect to the city and its architecture. As such, it represents the highest expression of a tradition mostly found in a culture's monumental buildings. In the classical and traditional mind, the future and the past are part of a continuum. Tradition is a way of life that embodies the principle of sustainability. The ever-changing character of classical and traditional architecture reflects the changes in architectural and urban elements and reminds us of our debt to the past. We could think of tradition as the projection of society's highest aspirations into the future thus ensuring the best and perhaps the most sustainable aspects of a culture endure. Tradition is not duplication but rather a process that is always inventing upon itself. It is the inventive quality of tradition that allows each generation to shape the future in its own manner and it is tradition's projection of the past that provides the sense of stewardship that is required for sustainability.

Thus the Richard H. Driehaus Prize is a recognition of optimism, an optimism embedded in principles of sustainability that promises a bright future for humanity. This optimism comes from a grounding in humanist values and education. In contrast to contemporary attitudes about art and architecture that celebrate the found object or a personal style rooted in the latest emotive notions of an author, in the classical and traditional mind, art and architecture must come from values and knowledge found on many spectrums. Below are two such spectrums that have significance with respect to how we can reframe our worldview to be both inclusive and still allow for distinctiveness in our cultures.

One such spectrum is illustrated by typology and character, or how we see both unity and distinctiveness in the built environment. We are accustomed to think of history as a series of episodic ruptures mostly disconnected except for explanations of how one period led to another due to a series of specific events. Thus we conceive of the classical, the gothic, the renaissance, the baroque, and neo-classical as unique and separate. We also see various cultures as separate and distinct and we classify them in accordance with times and places. Thus, to our eye, a Chinese monumental building has nothing in common with a Greek temple. However, upon closer examination we see both have pitched roofs, entasis in their columns, and specific commonalities with respect to intercolumniation. That there are cultural and historical exigencies that separate these places and times may be true, but more important are the continuities that thread them together and illustrate the universality of the human condition.

In contrast, the modernist ideology assumes one size fits all. Hong Kong resembles Vancouver, Doha resembles Cape Town, and London's East End resembles Santiago. The glass buildings are built indiscriminately without regard to climate or place. Such an attitude reduces the sense of place and disregards any economies that are gained by building structures whose materials come from the region in which they are built and are designed to perform optimally for their environment.

Another spectrum is the relationship between the public and private realms. Humans are social creatures and find knowledge, economy, inspiration, comfort, and joy in the company of others. The opposite of our social nature is the need for privacy. We gain security, inspiration, and comfort in the privacy of our homes. We cannot be isolated for long periods of time and we need to return to our public realm after being recharged from isolation. Another part of the private realm has traditionally been that commerce, until the twentieth century, was largely the domain of individuals. The need for identity, to compete and vie for supremacy, is as much a part of the human condition as the need for collaboration and cooperation. The city with its public and private spaces facilitates this dual and dissimilar nature. The private realm is represented by two types of buildings in the ideal city—the residential fabric of a city that offers privacy and shelter and the commercial entities that offer the competitive and individual enterprises that foster cultural vitality. The public realm is made up of capital buildings, town halls, libraries, schools, and other public institutions that both celebrate the accomplishments of a culture and facilitate its governance education and broader cultural aspirations.

With respect to buildings, walls give us privacy and identity; openings modulate the relationship of a space to the outside world. Thus bathrooms and kitchens have small windows on one end of the spectrum, living rooms and libraries have large ones on the other, and colonnades and arcades—which could be seen as walls with as much of the material removed as possible— make the most porous connection between public spaces such as streets and the spaces behind them. Together at both the scales of urbanism and architecture, the city, with its streets, squares and blocks, and architecture with its walls, openings, and roofs, facilitate the delicate balance between our public and private natures—the need for individual aspirations and the community that fulfills our common purposes.

In contrast, the modernist city is full of forms that belong to the private realm. The zoned existence of the typical sprawling suburb is a clear illustration of how the public realm has been replaced by the private realm with gated communities and shopping malls that have overshadowed the main streets of America and the rest of the world. Architectural form is more likely to come from the emotive reflexes of a starchitect than reflect a hierarchy of civic purpose, shared understandings of form, as well as the talent of the architect steeped in knowledge of his or her art.

In the brave new world of techno-utopia solutions, problems beget larger problems. For example, hybrid cars may be more efficient but the embodied energy in the batteries probably offsets any savings to the planet. It is true that we cannot live like we did in the eighteenth century but it is also impossible to continue living with the model of consumption and waste that cheap energy has given us. The humanist cities of the past were built in good times and in bad but always with a sense of conservation and investment.

Modern architecture trades on momentary emotions, on fads that produce shock and awe, but often stand in opposition to society's values, which are the currency of permanence. Without attention to those values, today's attraction becomes tomorrow's eyesore. Modern blight and excess create more than an aesthetic problem. The built environment is the single largest contributor to the climate change that threatens our planet. Sprawl and the urge to replace, rather than reuse, buildings that have no cultural significance take a social and environmental toll that we can no longer afford to pay. The debts of nations pale in comparison to the debt of our poorly planned built environment.

Traditional building techniques take little from the earth, producing no toxic chemicals and no waste. In this way, the architects the Driehaus Prize honors display their optimism for the future. They look forward, advocating modest consumption of the earth's resources, at once following the example that has worked for centuries with the courage to lead its renaissance in the contemporary world.

Léon Krier was the inaugural Driehaus Prize laureate because he started this discussion back in the 1970s. His advocacy and example, shared by many of our winners and extending to the generations that follow, transcends cultures. That has been an important facet of the Driehaus Prize, recognizing architects around the world, who represent diverse points of view and expressions while sharing a larger vision that animates the broader mission of this modern movement.

The Driehaus laureates' work has also included experiments on how to incorporate new as well as old technologies. Robert A.M. Stern and Demetri Porphyrios, while devoted to principles of traditional urbanism and architecture, have also taken some risks with modern curtain wall construction in an attempt to link it back to a coherent language, while Abdel-Wahed El-Wakil, Rafael Manzano Martos, and Quinlan Terry have renewed the application of load bearing masonry construction in both monumental and vernacular settings. Jaquelin Robertson and Andrés Duany and Elizabeth Plater-Zyberk have looked at the city as a whole while Michael Graves reestablished a clear dialogue with the past in the evolution of his work that inspired modern architecture to return to classical compositional rules and forms.

The laureates our jury has selected make up a constellation in the sky, each a shining light in their own right, but together illuminating a larger view of the world. Made up of world leaders in their fields, the jury has combined grand ideas and visions to offer a glimpse as to how to shape our future. Year after year, it has become clear there are different components to the classical idea. The work of the Driehaus laureates comes from all corners of the earth, engages new and old technologies to offer the lowest energy consumption and maximize conservation, and restores the city to a place where the private and public realms are visible and celebrated.

The mission has never been narrow, a mere opportunity for classicists to pat other classicists on the back. The Prize has credibility across a range of architectural philosophies, as it must to make a meaningful impact on the contemporary world and serve the future as we intend. What we celebrate in these pages, and in the shadow of the great buildings and urban environments our laureates have designed, is not just a love of Classicism or traditional architecture, but a commitment to making those principles meaningful in contemporary life to build a sustainable future.

LÉON
KRIER

2003 Laureate

A Cultural Foundation

Why I practice Traditional Architecture and Urbanism

I grew up in an environment that, despite two recent world wars, was unblemished by Modernist architecture and planning. Until the mid-1960s, Luxembourg was a miracle of traditional architecture, a small capital city of 70,000 souls, embedded in manicured agricultural and horticultural landscapes and lofty beach forests. We lived on a tree-lined corniche, overlooking a deep valley and one of the most accomplished townscapes in Europe. My father's tailoring workshop occupied the ground floor of the townhouse, and for my primary education I hopped across the street when the school bells chimed. I had most of my secondary education in the baroque abbey of Echternach, a small medieval town, which together with its four-towered Romanesque Basilica had, in less than ten years, been beautifully reconstructed in a hundred percent artisan way after near total destruction during the 1944 Rundstedt offensive.

My parents regularly took their four children to Switzerland, France, and Italy to visit places of beauty. In front of the Jungfrau, the panorama of Florence, or the lakefront of Lugano, we experienced an aesthetic communion of awe and admiration. The family concord shattered when I chose a destination, taking my parents in 1963 to see Le Corbusier's *Cité Radieuse*. Though I didn't realize it immediately, that visit defined my life's orientation.

Until then, I had, via my brother, become acquainted with Modernism merely through books of Le Corbusier, Giedion, and Gropius. The formidable promises expressed there had swollen my sails. I imagined modernist architecture to be superior to all the beautiful buildings I had seen. I fantasized of white Cubist volumes adorning my favorite places and mile-long inhabited walls, plowing across Luxembourg's historic city center, bridging its valleys and digging into its ramparts and forested hillsides—radiant visions of an unearthly splendor. Before the ill-fated visit we camped in an uncle's

Atlantis at Sunrise. Painting by Carl Laubin. Léon Krier with Robert Day.

olive grove in Provence, enjoying perfectly intact beaches, towns, and landscapes. The timeless perfection of a nearby Cistercian monastery, the picturesque charm of the surrounding farms and hill towns, and not least our bloated expectations for the impending Marseille visit had indeed ill-prepared us for the tawdry reality of the *Cité Radieuse*. We were all speechless with shock, wondering at first whether we were at the right address.

The relentless modernist devastation of Luxembourg, which started in full a few years later, not only alienated me from my cherished birthplace, but more radically from Modernism, the intellectual homeland in which I had sought temporary refuge from a provincial upbringing. I took it personally and decided to fight back, not clearly knowing who the enemy was.

Unable to find a master, a school, or a doctrine that could teach me how to stop the destruction and learn my craft, I felt I had no choice but to learn from the buildings, towns, and landscapes that my family and I had experienced and loved. I decided to abandon university, to think, to draw, and to generally find out what was so wrong with contemporary architecture and urbanism and how to right it—not because I felt I had a special gift in that direction, but because of a realization that nobody else, not even those I most esteemed, seemed inclined to do what I felt had to be done.

To me the worst consequences of Modernism lie not only in the worldwide degeneration of the general building activity through the loss of traditional building technology and skills, but more tragically in the intellectual corruption of their forms of transmission and theoretical foundations. Modernism's historicization of traditional architectures, i.e. the ideologically-motivated reduction of a timeless building technology to a mere collection of obsolete styles and crafts, has blinded several generations to the continuing modernity and irreplaceable value of classical architecture and traditional practices.

The universal principles of traditional architecture—firmness, utility, harmony—are concordant with the fundamental goals of all significant human establishments. In all great cultures they have been the chosen means of wise policy and civilizing action. In the whirlwind of all things human, they have been the guarantors of social bond stability and peace, the visible realization of a common moral world.

LONG-TERM INVESTMENT

The most important struggle in architecture today is not between Tradition and Modernism, but between true and false traditional building construction. Almost everywhere the building industry has abandoned load-bearing construction in favor of a separation of support-structure and external enclosure and, secondly, replaced natural building materials by industrial substitutes. The incongruous mixing of materials and techniques, the reduction of external walls to screens, the tireless differential movements between structure and enclosure, and lastly the substitution of synthetic for natural materials makes even traditional-looking buildings into extremely vulnerable, high-maintenance structures of limited life expectancy. It also turns most traditionally-styled buildings into authentic fakes, of traditional appearance only, resulting almost unavoidably in post-modernist kitsch.

Against the mere skin depth of most post-modernist buildings, true vernacular and classical structures are wall-deep and room-deep. Authentic traditional construction and the predominant

Campanile and Village Hall, Windsor, Florida, acrylic.

use of natural materials are essential to ensure the integrity of structure, architectural elements, and appearance. A slightly higher initial investment is repaid by a longer life, by less maintenance, better appearance, and generally better building.

Buildings ought not to be conceived as objects of short-term consumption but of long-term use. The principles that guide their design and construction must therefore transcend fashions and whims. Paraphrasing political theorist Hannah Arendt, without buildings and towns transcending the lifespan of their builders, no public realm, no lasting and collective expression in craft or art form, strictly speaking, no culture is possible.

The classical triad of *firmitas-utilitas-venustas* has meaning in a long-term perspective only. There is no more short-term beauty than there is short-term wisdom. Even the most solid and practical structure has a futile destiny if it lacks beauty. Solidity and permanence, utility and commodity, and beauty and harmony are unconditionally interdependent and their links are severed in Modernism. This is why timeless or traditional principles are in irreconcilable contradiction with time-bound or Modernist principles.

Pizza Metafisica.

Opposite:
Cittá Nuova Urban Center, Alessandria, Italy. Léon Krier and Gabriele Tagliaventi.

Many critics still want to see the competition between Classicism and Modernism as an ideological struggle to the death. This clearly reveals a pre-democratic frame of mind because its eradication from professional education and practice has not and will not eliminate the need for classical architecture. It has, however, ensured that for sixty years classical designers had no chance to gain public commissions. It has also secured for at least two generations the practice of the most debased Classicism ever. Furthermore, the brutality of Modernism is at its most extreme when and where it reigns supreme. Not by chance did Modernism produce its best results when it was a minority exercise in the 1920s. The renewed competition is now improving the products of both recent Modernism and Classicism.

The question can therefore no longer be Tradition versus Modernism but democratic competition, a high level of education and professional practice in all disciplines, and nonpartisan criticism. The real struggle to the death is between good and bad design.

Bicentennial plan for the completion of the Federal City, Washington, D.C. Commissioned by Arthur Drexler, M.O.M.A. New York.

Masterplan for Cayalá, Guatemala City, Guatemala. Léon Krier, Richard Economakis and Estudio Urbano.

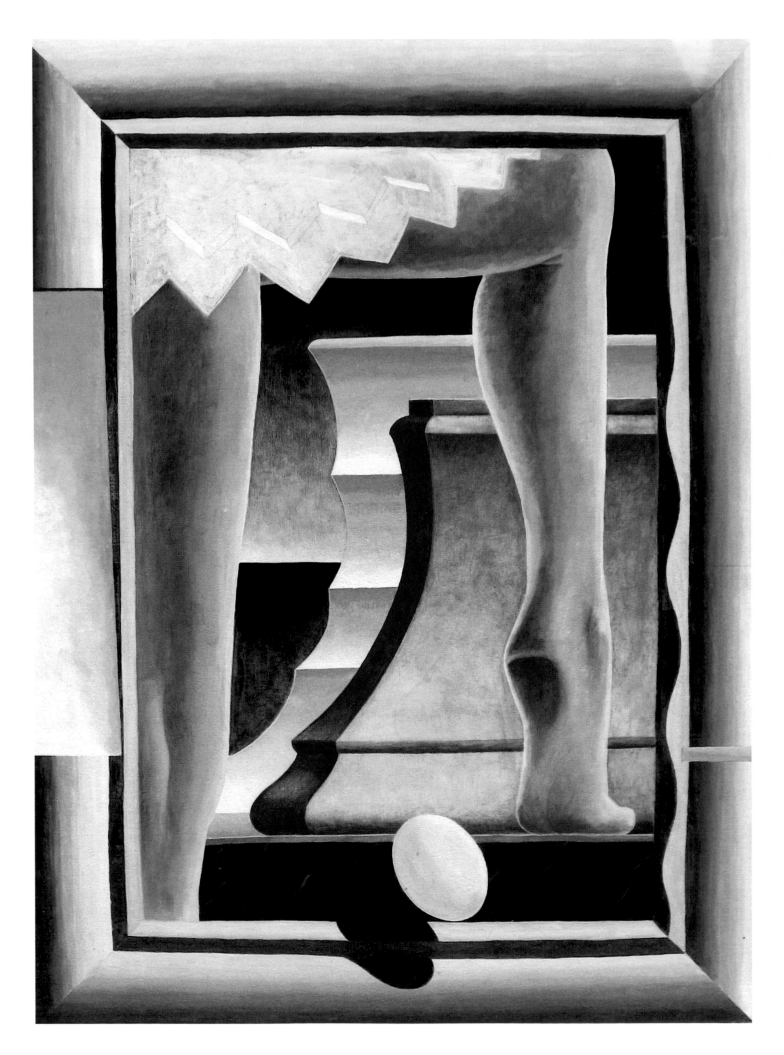

Krier House, Seaside, Florida.

Opposite:
Analytique, Acrylic Painting.

Aerial View of Middle Farm Quarter, Poundbury, Dorset, England. Masterplan.

Opposite: Queen Mother Square Tower, Poundbury, Dorset, England. Léon Krier and Colum Mulhern.

Masterplan for Tor Bella Monaca, Rome, Italy. Redevelopment plan for first phase. Léon Krier, Christiano Rosponi and Jamshid Sepehri.

Opposite: Vista towards Torre Mercato. Tor Bella Monaca, Rome, Italy.

Village Hall and Fountain,
Windsor, Florida.
Léon Krier with Merrill Pastor.

Highgrove Garden Chair for HRH The Prince of Wales.

Opposite: The Jorge Perez Architecture Centre, University of Miami. Léon Krier, Merrill Pastor and Ferguson Glasgow Schuster Soto, Inc.

DEMETRI
PORPHYRIOS

2004 Laureate

The Relevance of the Classical

It is in buildings, better than in anything else we create, that we can sense a vivid awareness of the gap between the absolute—that which ought to be—and our limited human reason to grasp it. Both public and intensely private, architecture's paramount interest has always been and continues to be the tectonic narrative of shelter. I have always maintained that buildings should look natural, unaffected, as if nothing else could have been built instead. It is only then that buildings can converse with their neighbors, honor their forefathers, but also swerve away from tradition exactly because they belong to a tradition. Character, therefore, relates to propriety. On one end of the spectrum is vernacular; on the other is the classical. The first is fuelled by necessity; the second is inspired by the struggle of humanism to come to terms with the absolute.

This is the sense in which we can say that Classicism is *not* a style. It is important to remember that the classical relates form to use but also to construction and shelter. The classical naturalizes the principles of shelter by turning them into myth: the demarcations of beginning and ending are commemorated as base and capital; the experience of load-bearing is made perceptible through the entasis in the shaft of the column; the chief beam, binding the columns together and imposing on them a common load, becomes the architrave; the syncopation of the transversal beams resting on the architrave is rendered visible in the figures of the triglyphs and metopes of the frieze; the projecting rafters of the roof, supported by the frieze, appear in the form of the cornice; finally and most significantly—the whole tectonic assemblage of column, architrave, frieze, and cornice becomes the ultimate object of classical contemplation in the idea of Order.

The Order sets form over the necessities of shelter; it sets the artifice of the tectonic over the contingencies of construction. The power of formal artifice presides. The possibility of creating such a formal artifice constitutes the prime aesthetic subject matter of classical thought. Classical architecture constructs a tectonic artifice out of the productive level of building. The artifice of constructing this world is seen as analogous to the artifice of constructing the human

Whitman College, Princeton University, New Jersey.

world. In its turn, myth allows for a convergence of the real and the fictive so that the real is redeemed. By rendering construction and shelter mythically fictive, classical thought posits reality in a contemplative state, wins over the depredations of petty life and, in a moment of rare disinterestedness, rejoices in the power it has over contingent life.

That is what makes us call classical whatever is retrieved from the vicissitudes of changing time and changing taste. That is why the term classical always points to something enduring, with a significance that is independent of all circumstances of time. In those things we name classical we recognize a kind of timeless present that is contemporaneous and at ease with every historical period.

A work is classical not because its meaning is perpetuated but because it continually invites commentary and ferrets out the new. The classical reaches across culture and time and, taking the risk of anachronism, it heals the estrangement which humanism constantly faces. The classical, then, is certainly the enduring and timeless. But this timelessness always takes the form of modernity; that is, it takes the form of the relevance of tradition.

Private Residence,
Kensington, London.

Opposite:
Duncan Galleries,
Lincoln, Nebraska.

Right:
Detail of Pergola, Private
Residence, Town of Pitiousa,
Spetses, Greece.

Below:
Highbury Gardens, Islington,
London. (Photo: Hufton+Crow)

Opposite top:
Private Residence, Porto, Heli,
Greece.

Opposite bottom:
Town of Pitiousa, Spetses, Greece.

Overleaf:
Ann's Court, Selwyn College,
Cambridge, England.

Belvedere Village, Ascot, England.

Opposite:
Whitman College, Princeton
University, Princeton, New Jersey.

Right:
Detail, Interamerican
Headquarters Office Building,
Athens, Greece.

Below:
Duncan Galleries, Lincoln,
Nebraska.

Opposite:
Interamerican Headquarters
Office Building, Athens, Greece.

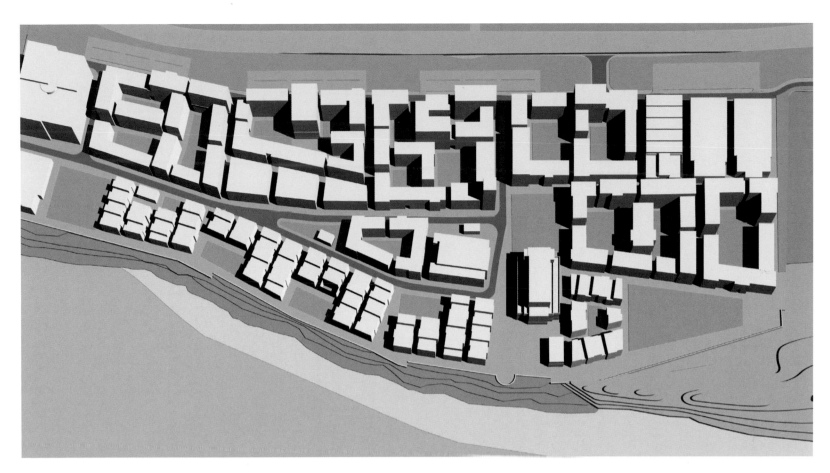

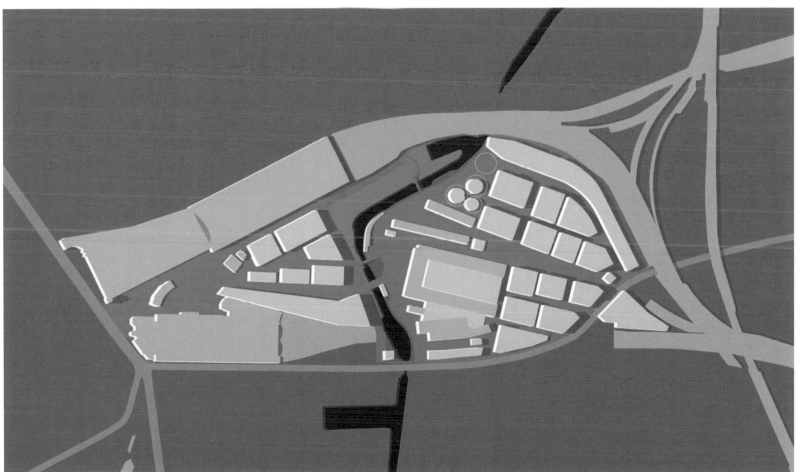

Above: Kings Cross Central Masterplan, Kings Cross, London.   Opposite: Rocco Forte Villa Kennedy Hotel, Frankfurt, Germany.

Top: The Bay Campus Masterplan, Swansea University, Wales, England.   Overleaf: Whitman College, Princeton University, New Jersey.

QUINLAN
TERRY

2005 Laureate

The Expression of Civilization

There are many ways to describe classical architecture today but clearly it should be more than a Corinthian column tacked on to a steel frame or a tempietto on top of a skyscraper. It is much deeper than that.

Classical architecture is primarily the right way to build a permanent structure in traditional materials with a preference for using brick, stone, lime mortar, timber and pitched roofs covered in slate or tile. It is working within the disciplines of solid load-bearing masonry construction with all that implies: a limit in height, a preoccupation with the size and position of windows to provide comfortable conditions within the building, a natural bias towards simple solid geometry, a willingness to use ornament, and a desire to express the classical orders in all their fullness as they are appropriate to the fabric of the building and its neighbors.

The classical architecture that we admire in Rome, Paris, London lasts for centuries, whereas modern architecture lasts for a few decades. When all of the prosperity which we have been living on for the last sixty years begins to tumble we shall be grateful that we live in a building that is traditional and therefore can be repaired, rather than a modern building in which the simplest thing is to pull it down and start again. In short, we should carry on the great classical tradition of our forefathers.

Alongside this, we should—and will soon *have to*—consider a more modest consumption of the earth's resources to service our buildings. The classical tradition developed over thousands of years in ages which had no elevators, no electric light, no air conditioning, and yet they lived and prospered in all climates, took little out of the earth, produced no toxic chemicals and no waste—everything was recycled. Classical architecture is a tradition that has worked and would go on providing a sustainable environment if we would have the courage to follow that example. Only in this way will we produce buildings which are both beautiful to behold and not harmful to the environment.

Tuscan Villa, Regents Park, London. (Photo: Nick Carter)

Overleaf:
Baker Street Development, London. (Photo: Neil Waving)

Left: Baker Street Development, London. (Photo: by Neil Waving)

Above: Richmond Riverside Development, Surrey, England. (Photo: by Claude Mercier)

Architects are a major cause of the problem that cannot be solved by homage to environmental issues with flow diagrams showing air movements. Many buildings, particularly skyscrapers, are environmental disasters. Over the last sixty years architects have built cities totally dependent on steel, reinforced concrete, and plastics. Architects think nothing of burning up the earth's resources to service our buildings, which become higher, wider, and deeper—all more dependent on artificial light, air conditioning, and elevators. With profligate use of oil and gas we design temporary buildings of inferior materials that have to be replaced at regular intervals. We have therefore produced an unsustainable and precarious environment.

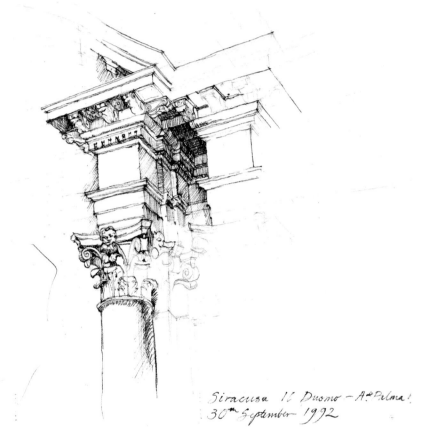

Siracusa Il Duomo – A.P.Palma
30th September 1992

SO WHERE DO WE GO FROM HERE?

Traditional building construction is the alternative that has worked and proved worthy over thousands of years, using solid masonry, modest height, pitched slate and tile roofs, smaller windows. It is beautiful and sustainable. It is the architectural expression of every civilized age. But is has now been rejected.

To reverse this current trend will require a life of painstaking labor, commitment, and dedication to achieve even modest satisfaction—and I have to acknowledge that even then I seldom reach a level worthy of comparison with the architectural achievements of our forefathers.

This process is doubly difficult in our generation because of the attractions of an alternative way of building which can provide structures that are higher, cheaper, lighter, and quicker to erect. Such buildings are less permanent—have no beauty or charm, and are wholly dependent on high consumption of energy to survive. However, with the exception of a handful of institutions like the University of Notre Dame School of Architecture, they have captivated the minds of virtually all the

Il Duomo. Siracuse
30 Sept 1992
Arch. Andrea di Palma
1754

academies, seats of learning, and leaders of the architectural establishment. It means that anyone who wants to pursue contemporary Classicism seriously will have to plow a lonely furrow, enduring conflict, obloquy, and insults throughout their career.

In my case I have had to fight every step of the way for the last fifty years against entrenched opposition with the architectural establishment, not to mention closet modernists in the conservation bodies. I have survived because I have been fortunate to have been commissioned by those independently minded clients looking for a long-term solution to an age old problem. I have also had the support of friends and patrons.

As we think of patrons we should remember how crucial they have been at critical points in the history of architecture. There would hardly have been a Renaissance without a Medici or the Farnese. Without the vision of Julius II we would not have heard of Michelangelo, Bramante, Sangallo, or Vignola. Without John D. Rockefeller, Jr. we would have hardly heard of Colonial Williamsburg.

In that tradition, Richard Driehaus's encouragement and support is crucial for the revival and survival of architecture today. The Richard H. Driehaus Prize at the University of Notre Dame gives the whole movement of traditional architecture more of a voice and more prestige and more importance.

But—dare I say it?—there is something even more significant! Classical architecture like all the fine arts, music and poetry runs parallel with our Judeo-Christian heritage where the past is in front of us and the future behind us; an idea now so alien to our generation which is busily editing history out of its education system and so besotted with the hopes and fears, plans and projections of the future. The Word of Life insists that concerning the future we know nothing except the single fact that one day we shall meet our Maker, either at our death or his return; by contrast the past in all its glittering variety spreads before those who are prepared to see, a comprehensive guide to living in the meantime.

Opposite: Francis and Quinlan Terry sketching in Ascoli Piceno, Italy.
(Photo: Christine Terry)

Above: Corinthian Villa, Regents Park, London.
(Photo: Nick Carter)

Richmond Riverside Development, Surrey, England. (Photo: June Buck)

Doorway, St. Helen's,
Bishopsgate, City of London.
(Photo: Nick Carter)

Opposite:
Maitland Robinson Library,
Downing College,
Cambridge, England.
(Photo: Nick Carter)

Brentwood Cathedral, Essex, England.
(Photo: Nick Carter)

Overleaf:
Colonial Williamsburg, Virginia.
(Photo: Colonial Williamsburg
Foundation, Barbara Lombardi)

ALLAN
GREENBERG

2006 Laureate

Declarations of Independence

In the late 1950s I was an architectural student in South Africa. Not long out of high school, I was perusing the pages of the Italian journal, L'Architettura, and became interested in a vituperative debate between Rayner Banham and Bruno Zevi about the Neo-Liberty architectural movement– a group of young Italian architects inspired by Art Nouveau. The discussion abruptly ended when Zevi, editor of L'Architettura, published a full-page photograph of a sublimely beautiful Art Nouveau door handle by Victor Horta. The page heading was "Riposta a Banham." How could Banham respond to this challenge? For the first time I understood, viscerally as well as intellectually, that great architecture speaks with its own authority. Even an ordinary door handle can move the observer into a realm beyond words, into the unique world of architectural form.

At his inauguration as third president of the United States in 1801, Thomas Jefferson spoke these words, "Every difference of opinion is not a difference of principle. We have called by different names brethren of the same principle. We are all republicans, we are all federalists."

I say to you that we are all modernists and we are all classicists. But more important, we are all architects. And on the Day of Judgment, the only question the muse of architecture will ask us is whether our work is good or whether it is something else.

I have been an architect for fifty years and, at this point in my life, I know only two things for certain: that I don't know all that much, and that architecture seems to become ever more difficult.

As I assembled these thoughts, I was looking out from my 20th floor apartment on Third Avenue in New York City. The mediocrity of most of the surrounding post-1950 buildings is overwhelming.

Humanities Building, Rice University, Houston, Texas.

Similar buildings can be found in Shanghai, Moscow, Johannesburg, Berlin, and London. They are alienated from local culture, climate, and geography. Surely our great cities like New York, Chicago, San Francisco, and Washington, D. C. deserve better from their architects.

Henry Glassie, who documented the vernacular architecture of Virginia and other places, said, "Buildings, like poems and rituals, realize culture. Their designers rationalize their actions differently. Some say they design and build as they do because it is the ancient way of their people and place. Others claim that their practice correctly manifests the universal laws of science. But all of them create out of the smallness of their own experience."

By focusing on the smallness of our own experience and on the context of our hometowns, we can create architecture that grows directly out of our physical, social, psychological, and emotional needs—an anthropomorphic and anthropocentric architecture whose strands are woven around the rhythms of our daily lives. And this architecture will also be rooted in the deepest strands of our identity as a people.

A good measure of who we are may be our choice of references: the buildings we love, study, and emulate. My first heroes were Frank Lloyd Wright, Le Corbusier, and Edwin Lutyens. Fifty years later my heart still quickens when I see photographs of Taliesin West, the Villa Savoye, or the Viceroy's House, now the President's official residence in New Delhi. Confronted by such greatness, who cares about ideological differences? I am equally passionate about the great architects of the past like Ictinus, who designed the Parthenon and the temple of Apollo at Bassae, and Mnesicles, who created the Propylea, or gateway to the Acropolis. Surely their work moved the muse of architecture to smile.

I have sketched Michelangelo's buildings until I know them by heart. And Thomas Jefferson, our greatest architect, took my hand and led me through his buildings, explaining the intimate links between the political and architectural aspirations of the early Republic. And, for the last decade, I have been obsessed with the buildings of Francesco di Giorgio and Henry Hobson Richardson. Their forms are permeated by a spirit that is eternal yet also projects a sense of something raw and archaic, of ideas cut close to the edge. They emanate a rare quality that Plato called "sacred fear."

In New York, where I now spend most of my time, I marvel at the genius of Rockefeller Center, the city's noblest urban space; and the Empire State Building, which will always be tallest because it is the very best skyscraper ever built. Where else could Tom Hanks and Meg Ryan meet, or King Kong climb to his sad and inevitable end? And I ask you, are these two works of architecture classical or modern? I don't think it matters. They are both classical and modern; and they are both masterpieces.

We should base our architecture on ideas more profound than the current oppositions of classical and modern, of tradition and innovation. That debate is about style and opinion. If we are going to have divisions, let them be about matters of substance, like freedom and tyranny. I also believe that we, those of us interested in using history as an integral part of

Walkway, Humanities Building, Rice University, Houston, Texas.

architectural design, should reclaim the word modern. The very concept of modernity, as Charles Baudelaire explained nearly 150 years ago, incorporates both the ephemeral and the eternal. In order to be radically new you have to be conscious of what came before. Our architecture should be so inclusive and so encompassing that it has a place for classical, gothic, vernacular, and modernistic design.

My own buildings grow out of my passion for American architecture. This story starts at the end of August 1964, when I arrived in the United States accompanied by my wife and two very small children. Standing in the main concourse of the International Terminal at John F. Kennedy Airport in New York, I heard English spoken with more accents than I had ever imagined existed. I felt an electric energy pulsing through the ground where I stood. At that moment I fell in love with America and I knew I had come home.

That passion has intensified during the five decades I have lived here. Through hard times and good times, I never failed to be touched by the warmth and generosity of Americans from all walks of life. I fled South Africa because of its apartheid system. Like so many who came here from lands steeped in oppression, I remain awed by the American political system. An avid reader of American history, I have long regarded the nation's founding documents—the Declaration of Independence, the Constitution, and the Bill of Rights—as miraculous creations, on the order of the tablets of the law that God handed Moses. But these remarkable legal documents were authored by human beings as a part of their struggle against injustice. One of my great pleasures is to sit in the library at my office and page through the correspondence of George Washington or Thomas Jefferson, to open a biography of James Madison, or to read the opinions of John Marshall or the speeches of Abraham Lincoln.

And I am equally moved by our vernacular architecture, by the creative drive of the nameless owner-builders, carpenters and masons who were the architects of colonial and nineteenth-century America. Their consistently inventive work sings of the aspirations of a free people. And it is this drive towards freedom that also inspired the architecture and city planning of Jefferson, Latrobe, Thornton, Washington, Bulfinch and L'Enfant. These ideals speak directly to us, to our clients, and to the public about matters that are more profound and more pressing than arcane debates about stylistic preference and theories of design. American architecture should be rooted in our dreams for freedom, civil rights and equality, and for the delicate balance of power that permits these ideals to thrive.

My passion for American architecture, for the architecture of democratic Athens and republican Rome, for the buildings of the Florentine republic established in 1290, and seventeenth-century Holland and England continues to grow. This architecture is important for its political content, and for the innovative ways its architects articulated these ideals in brick and mortar.

While living in Guilford, Connecticut I participated in town meetings. For someone from South Africa, where two-thirds of the population had no say in the government, the experience was profound. Our town hall was a nondescript building, but when I visited seventeenth- and early eighteenth-century Puritan meetinghouses in New England, I felt a visceral link across 300 years with the settlers who first voted to plan their community's future.

Faculty Office Wing,
Humanities Building,
Rice University, Houston, Texas.

In 1966 I visited Jefferson's masterwork, the University of Virginia. The Academical Village is an expression of democratic and republican ideals, and its architecture is Jefferson's eloquent description of a community dedicated to learning. It is more than an assembly of classrooms, dormitories, dining halls, and laboratories. It is an expression of the role of education in a democracy.

I arrived at my particular Rubicon in 1976. My first two projects were complete. The first was an addition to the Connecticut State Library and Supreme Court designed by Donn Barber in 1908. My addition to this beautiful classical building was inspired by the work of Alvar Aalto and Gunnar Asplund. I planned an austere curved façade that deferred to the older building; its structural steel columns were set behind recessed limestone panels; and the large Swedish windows were double glazed, reversible for cleaning, and had blinds between the panes. The second was an addition to a late seventeenth-century Connecticut saltbox. I began with a design inspired by Marcel Breuer's early houses in Connecticut and Massachusetts. Unsatisfied by the lack of any formal or intellectual relationship between new and old, I experimented with a Shingle Style addition. In his great study of the Shingle Style, Vincent Scully described how H.H. Richardson sent Charles McKim, then a young architect in his office, to measure colonial houses in New England. Richardson was as interested in the lean-to additions in the rear as he was in the original house. My final design combined a lean-to roof in the manner of colonial additions to saltboxes and large windows inspired by Shingle Style houses. Assessing both my buildings, I decided that my Supreme Court wing, with its reliance on contrasting new and old, did not sustain the same intensity of discourse that took place between the saltbox and the lean-to addition.

At this time I was privileged to be teaching in the Yale Law School. During a conversation in the faculty lounge, a colleague stunned me by saying that, "there is no history of the law." In response to my blank stare, he explained that "the law is its own history. Through the case study method, and the methodical study of legal precedent, the past is always an integral part of the present and the future." I began to understand the far-reaching methodological implications of Walter Gropius's restructuring of architectural education at the Bauhaus and later at Harvard. He not only stopped teaching history, but changed design methodology by rejecting the use of precedent—both aesthetic and functional. For him and his disciples and descendants, history and the past are, and still remain, irrelevant.

I loved the intimate engagement with history I experienced designing my modest addition to the Connecticut saltbox. I began to understand how the history of architecture could be integrated into its daily practice. This was how I wanted to practice architecture. Striking out in this direction determined the future course of my life.

In 2006, I published a book that strives to move beyond the dead end of classical versus modern, tradition versus new technology, vernacular versus zeitgeist. This book, *The Architecture of Democracy: American Architecture and the Legacy of the Revolution*, is my thank you to the people of the United States for their hospitality and for allowing me to come home.

Brooks Brothers Store,
Rodeo Drive,
Beverly Hills, California.

Private Residence, New Albany, Ohio.

Left and Above: Private Residence, New Albany, Ohio.

Overleaf left: George C. Marshall Reception Room, Offices of the Secretary of State, U.S. Department of State, Washington, D.C.

Overleaf right: Treaty Room, U.S. Department of State, Washington, D.C.

Above, Opposite and Overleaf: Restoration and addition, Private Residence, Greenwich, Connecticut.

JAQUELIN T. ROBERTSON

2007 Laureate

Architecture's Great Continuum

A traditionalist in retrospect, exposed since childhood to some of our country's best buildings and settings, I have also been caught up and interested in the modernist world. Indeed, I have not only designed modernist buildings of which I am proud, but there are modernist elements in a number of my traditional buildings and plans.

Simply put, I have been most interested in what Louis Kahn called the "great continuum" of architecture—the past in the present and vice versa. Western classicism is about that continuum, a constant, renewable language and energy source.

The continuity in the flow of certain ideas back and forth is true of all great architectural cultures. I have seen 500-year-old Persian villages in the desert more up-to-date ecologically, more suited to where they were, more beautiful than anything I have seen in the West in the last half of the twentieth century. They were at once modern and traditional, as "new" now as then.

All lasting architectures have a long genealogy and an interesting DNA, which not surprisingly, is different in each of the world's great cultures (e.g. China, Persia, India, Japan and so on). In the West, that family tree is about the evolution of Pan-Hellenic classicism and its many formal and vernacular regional offshoots that have spread across much of the world for over 2,000 years. If you go to the Dolomites, in Italy, and you go to Hokkaido, in Japan—totally different cultures, different races—how they build is remarkably the same, because the climate is the same, the materials they have to use are the same. And they figured out, over thousands of years, the best way to build in this climate with these materials.

New traditional communities with traditional buildings are being built here and abroad. The orders are once again being taught and traditional studios being given in the best schools. Prizes are being awarded, superb books written. All of which suggest that Western

Windsor Beach Club, Vero Beach, Florida. (Photo courtesy Windsor Beach Club)

classicism and traditional building is very much a part of the modern, if not the "modernist" world. If you took all the lists of qualities that people now employ for green architecture, modernist architecture almost meets none of them; whereas, traditional architecture almost meets all of them.

Why do cultures continue to return to these sources? Precisely because they remain the purest, deepest, and most refreshing of our architectural well springs. In essence, Western classicism is an ecology of ideas about architecture in which the underlying propositions are maintained as a result of continued flexibility among the variables. Its truths and processes are systemic and continue to evolve.

FROM ARISTOTLE TO YOGI BERRA

I was reminded recently by my partner Alex Cooper, of yet another of Yogi Berra's instructive pronouncements, "I came to the fork in the road ... and decided to take it."

The more I thought about this seeming absurdity—mumbling to myself, "Yes, of course"—the more I could visualize that fork in my road as a real but not-to-be-broken wishbone of connected interests that I had been drawn to early on and that had to do with two critical areas of human activity: Aristotle's *Poetics and Politics*, each informing and empowering the other, ineluctably conjoined.

The one, architecture—part art, part science, and part profession—establishes the physical setting for our lives and in so doing, gives perceptible meaning, value, and priority to our world. When done well, architecture is the most revealing and demanding of our arts. Because of its physicality it can't be avoided, and is our constant companion and a shaping presence, for better or worse.

The other area, the politics, in my case had to do with both the politics of design and the design of politics. How can one fashion and deliver—in a democratic, pluralistic, commercially driven culture—healthy settings that protect and enhance the natural world and are at once practical, elegant, just, and achievable?

It seemed to me that these two activities have never been trivial pursuits. Moreover, each one seeks balance—a balanced view of the world and of those around you. And in each, a combination of practicality, skill, and vision is needed to avoid the needless destruction of violent revolution. Thank God our Founding Fathers took as their preferred political model the Scottish Enlightenment and not the French Revolution, and that their preferred architectural model was Greece and Rome. Jefferson's Roman Revival was both grounded in the past and about the future. I believe that the United States benefited from carefully selected "lessons of the past" which we refitted for our future. Our form of government was both rooted and profoundly modern–my understanding, precisely, of tradition and modernity.

So how's that? Yogi Berra, Aristotle, Hume, Hutchison, Smith, Bogswell, and Jefferson all serving as markers for me. As they say, "If you want to see farther, you must stand on the shoulders of giants."

Front door, St. Luke's Parish House, Easthampton, New York. (Photo: Robert Benson)

Overleaf:
St. Luke's Parish Hall, Easthampton, New York. (Photo: Robert Benson)

RECOGNITIONS

My life and my views on architecture and politics have thus been shaped by people, places, institutions, idea systems, and the issues of the times, as well as by opportunities, connections, and good luck—exposures which have led to my own recognitions.

The issues of my times that have been most influential to what I was trying to do have to do with four things:

- The emergence of ecology and its implications for the planet. That is, how the world works. Think of Rachel Carson, Aldo Leopold, Gregory Bateson—profound teachers who changed both the way I thought and what I thought about.

- The increasing importance of historic preservation, of valued buildings and portions of our cities and our countrysides.

- The tragic loss of regionalism in architecture, planning, and place making. Different built settings in different parts of the world should look and work differently, but are increasingly the same.

- How and why modernist Western urbanism has been so destructive to cultures and valued built settings the world over.

These four critical interconnected issues have, until recently, gone largely unnoticed in our planning, development, and architectural strategies over the last fifty years. While we have had significant preservation victories, and seen the creation of regionally derived new places, we are still losing on ecology—which, increasingly, is the mega-issue facing the world today.

Ertegun House.
(Photo: Scott Frances / Esto)

Opposite:
Pool deck, Ertegun House.
(Photo: Elle Decoration /
Marianne Hass)

Overleaf:
Windsor Beach Club,
Vero Beach, Florida.
(Photo courtesy
Windsor Beach Club)

Right:
Aerial view, New Albany
Country Club, New Albany, Ohio.
(Photo: Top Site Aerial
Photography)

Opposite:
View from tennis court,
New Albany Country Club,
New Albany, Ohio.
(Photo: Robert Benson)

Below:
Elevation, New Albany Country
Club, New Albany, Ohio.
(Photo: Robert Benson)

Cerulean Park Water Course, WaterColor, Florida.

Opposite: Cerulean Park, WaterColor, Florida. (Photo: The St. Joe Company)

Entry Garden, Casa de Campo Villa, La Romana, Dominican Republic. (Photo: Steven Brooke)

Opposite: Great Hall interior, Casa de Campo Villa, La Romana, Dominican Republic. (Photo: Steven Brooke)

Adaptive reuse, Visitors' Reception and Transportation Centre, Charleston, South Carolina. (Photo: Robert Benson)

Previous spread: Golf clubhouse, Celebration, Florida. (Photo: Robert Benson)

East Hampton Cottage, Longdon Clay. (Photo: Langdon Clay)

ANDRES
DUANY

ELIZABETH
PLATER-ZYBERK

2008 Laureates

Expanding the Canon

Practicing traditional architecture and urbanism requires bravery because it means we enter the ring with champions like Lutyens and Palladio. Modernists write their own rules of the game, so they always win. Peter Eisenman, for example, is invariably the champion of Eisenman-esque architecture. There are no other contenders. This is clever, but in the end it is not interesting because all the thrilling tension is in his head. Eisenman's increasingly remarkable achievements hold our attention less every time. He does ever bigger buildings that are ever more swiftly catalogued away. They are victories over himself, about which only he can ultimately care.

But what if Peter were to design a classical building? What if he were to attempt something as dangerous as to contest the real champions? There would be a renewed interest in him as an architect, to say the least. And I'm sure it would be a great performance—Léon Krier, who is his friend, says Eisenman knows Palladio very well.

Designing a classical building is virtually the only thing that remains for those avant-garde architects. They have already explored every shape that could be levitated, crashed, randomized, perforated, photo-tuned, upturned, folded, dematerialized, dissed or otherwise transgressed. It is by now the expected. There remains only their engaging in the ultimate test, to compete with the likes of Lutyens and Palladio, under common rules.

But even that would be merely entertainment. For this dismal century before us, architecture and urbanism must be more useful than amusing.

Campo Sano Village, Coral Gables, Florida. (Photo: Raul Pedroso)

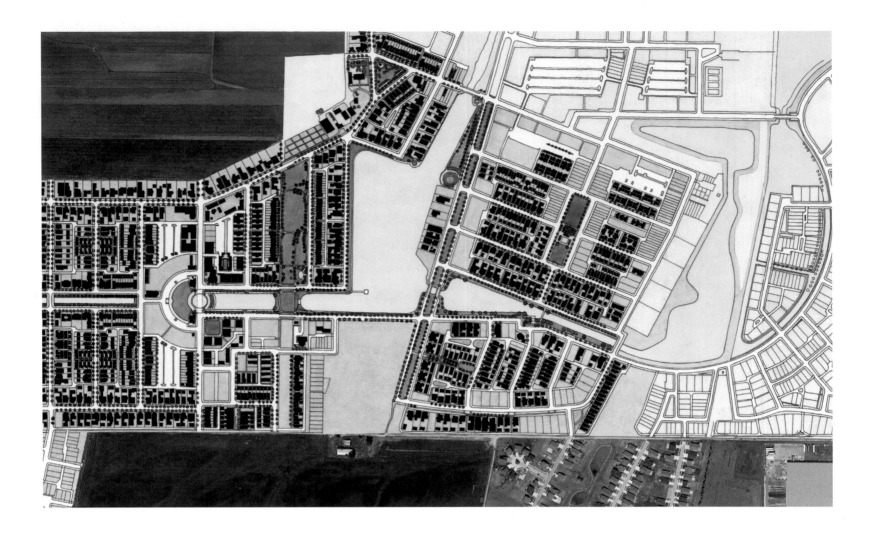

The current renaissance of traditional architecture must be seen not as a single event, but as a process. Classical architecture is built on tradition. Tradition tends to discard failure. It's almost a Darwinian process, that which succeeds continues and that which fails gets dropped. It has embedded within it a great deal of wisdom. The current generation can continue to unfurl beautiful banners from the ramparts, in the hopes that all will recognize its virtue—or it can sally to take territory by force. There is too much territory forlorn by American design. I do not allude to the bits held by Modernism, but to the vast areas held by mindless production builders, by the green gadgets that pass for environmental buildings, by the nauseating plan books, by the junk-space of civic buildings, by the junk-products at Home Depot, by the hapless mobile-home industry. These are blights on our physical and cultural landscape that can be redeemed only by traditional designers. This is risky, I know. We could jeopardize the impeccable reputation of the citadel; but we could also show the place that traditional architecture can hold as nothing else can.

In this quest, we must be as courageous as the generation of pioneers. Bob Stern, Jacque Robertson, Allan Greenberg, Tom Beeby, Rob Krier, Demetri Porphyrios, and Thomas Gordon Smith all risked their good names by entering the wilderness of postmodernism. But see what they gained on the other side: the architecture that we now so confidently reward with the Driehaus Prize.

The best proof that architecture has been well and truly recovered in that heroic thirty-year campaign is that it can be dependably taught. I am aware that the rigor of the classical canon enables

New Town St. Charles,
St. Charles, Missouri.

Above:
Master plan detail.

Opposite top:
Bungalow court.

Opposite bottom:
Aerial view.
(Photos: NTSC and
Whittaker Homes)

this instruction. I am also aware that the discipline of the Orders was the compass that guided architecture out of Postmodernism. But in teaching the Orders today we should take care that students do not become overly dependent on bookish authority. They must not learn the fear of being caught "incorrect." The measure should be what we call "plain old good architecture." After all, we are building primarily for the commons, not the patrons.

Will this generation bore deeper into refinement and elitism, or will it endeavor to spread classical architecture outwards to a broad, democratic, indeed populist, future? Will they continue reprinting ever more esoteric treatises, or will they write new ones conceived to serve, not the sixteenth or even the twentieth century, but the future which is upon us?

I would propose a new ethos—one no longer dedicated to the polishing of the classical canon of Vitruvius, Palladio, and Vignola, but to supplementing that canon. Because this process cannot be allowed to devolve into neo-postmodernist dissipation, it should still be based on the authority of masters and masterpieces. First we must transcend the closed historic treatises, to rescue that which was discarded in the reductive process of writing them. Then we must recover to our side those transitional nineteenth- and twentieth-century architects who have been assigned to the modernist camp—where they reside as the foundation of their authority—when they are, in fact, the last great flowering of Classicism.

Take Frank Lloyd Wright. You could see the Prairie School as the beginning of the fall, but you could also see it as the last of the Greek Revivals. Wright was among those who, instead of the Parthenon and all of its proprieties, took the Erechtheion and all of its freedoms, to extract a contemporary architecture. If the Erechtheion—its dynamic massing and multiple columniations, its agile engagement with topography, its free repertoire of moldings, its localized symmetries and rotated approaches, its complex, multi-leveled interior, its contradictions and unresolved tension— is classical, then Wright is certainly among the great masters of Classicism. Wright must be on our side if we are to take the territory of the twenty-first century.

Another master of the canon would be Jože Plečnik, who knew the classical language perfectly. Like Shakespeare, who found literature in moribund Latin and bequeathed it in native English with vitality to spare, Plečnik shows us the workings of what our brother Douglas Duany calls "the vernacular mind." Not "the vernacular," which is a style, but the vernacular mind, which is the way of folk art. It is the ability to compose from memory and circumstance, to work sequentially through anything and everything, with craft but not perfection. The folk tradition, which Plečnik brought to Classicism, is the essential tool to withstand the withering that the twenty-first century will impose upon us. Léon Krier knows it. Look at his American buildings at Miami, and at Seaside, and Windsor. What lessons do they hold? Not one of them is correct in the canonical sense, and yet they are canonical buildings. And so I would also bring into the canon the work of Léon Krier.

An expanded canon would include newly drawn plates alongside Vignola's: the Orders of masters such as Gilly, Soane, Thompson, Tony Garnier, Perret, Hoffmann, Loos, Asplund, Piacentini, Terragni, Stern, Graves, Porphyrios, Rob Krier. This treatise would claim an enormous amount of new territory for Classicism.

Fairchild Tropical Botanic Garden, Visitor Centre Ballroom, Coral Gables, Florida. (Photo: Robin Hill)

Overleaf:
Aqua, Miami Beach, Florida.
(Photo: Steven Brooke)

SUSTAINABILITY AND SUSTENANCE

Striving to make places of responsible character and beauty, we are all ravenous for knowledge. Eagerness to share experience is a hallmark of the New Urbanism. A cadre of thinkers and doers stimulates and prods us to be ambitious about our practice spanning the full range of human settlement concerns—smart growth, new urbanism, traditional and green building—addressing the seemingly ever-more contradictory goals of preserving environment, creating amenable social settings, and ensuring their long-term viability.

In retrospect it all adds up. We like to think of the work as a journey of enabling, starting with a new coastal vacation community in Florida. Without setting out to do so, Seaside showed a generation how traditional arrangements of streets and buildings produce a public realm that makes walking and knowing your neighbors desirable and fun. Seaside's early experiments in vernacular and classical building design seeded young architectural practices as well, advancing knowledge and experience in Classicism when there was still little such activity.

Numerous offspring followed, in unsuspecting places such as Gaithersburg (Kentlands), Louisville (Norton Commons), and St. Louis (New Town St. Charles). The new communities in turn influenced a series of experimental initiatives:

- The rebuilding of an inner-city neighborhood (Cleveland Central) encouraged the U.S. Department of Housing and Urban Development to reconsider its public-housing holdings and develop the Hope VI program.

- The establishment of an organization to convene the like-minded, the Congress for the New Urbanism (CNU), now in its fifteenth year, has consolidated and empowered shared values and principles of community building.

- The organizing of CNU's post-disaster urban design and building proposals in Mississippi and Louisiana, including the Katrina Cottage, resulted in new methods and new products, and even a federal agency's acknowledgment of the error of its trailer ways.

- The integration of a twentieth-century subtropical city's modernist architectural expression with traditional urbanism in a Miami Beach neighborhood called Aqua has broadened the audience of architects.

- In the South Dade Agriculture Study, economic data provided a rationale and a prototypical method for saving metropolitan farmland from development, setting the stage for new approaches such as agricultural urbanism.

- A continuing engagement with the civic leaders of Rhode Island's historic state capital, Providence, offers encouragement for other rustbelt revivals.

- The rewriting of the voluminous zoning code of Miami, a growing Sun Belt city, calls attention

Loreto Bay, Loreto, Mexico.

Overleaf:
Redevelopment, East Beach,
Norfolk, Virginia.
(Photo courtesy East Beach)

to the importance of building façade for the urban pedestrian experience and the ultimate goal to reduce vehicle dependence.

- The shepherding of a university architecture faculty of autonomous agendas in a shared context of pedagogy proffers an alternative to the fragmented architectural academy.

- And not least, the University of Miami commissioning of a Léon Krier confection that has campus-wide users standing in line to reserve dates at the Jorge M. Perez Architecture Center.

This has been a privileged trajectory and a storied battleground, bolstered by what many have taught us, to learn from history and to seek the rational in design and building, and sometimes, if appropriate, in not building. There is always the goal of emulating and reproducing the livability and grace of places that still exist to teach us—like Ortigia, where the marks of culture across the centuries, Phoenician, Greek, Roman, Arabic, French and Italian, provide an example of how we might enrich our own cities over time, with diversity that allows each expression its own place of integrity.

In both worlds, academia and practice, we hope that we have contributed to the shaping of urban environments that welcome the cultural elevation this prize supports. But while the battle continues, new challenges loom. In the growing popular focus on the health of the planet and its inhabitants, designers devoted to the evolution of Tradition and Classicism must emphasize their role. In the two essential responses to climate change—mitigation and adaptation—we architects and urban designers are positioned to implement both. The mitigation mandate of reduced carbon emissions through green building and compact urbanism is a universal agenda. Those who are versed in the principles of design predating the discovery of oil and electricity are well positioned to advance it and should not be shy in articulating their approach. The adaptation to environmental change such as sea-level rise requires a regional and local approach, a new kind of civic engagement in public consensus building in order to effectively address problems and their solutions. Architects with an irrefutable knowledge base are likewise well suited for this.

The elements of Classicism and the opportunity to continue developing the classical language is important today precisely because it represents our history. It represents the history of a culture, of a civilization. Recognizing the continuity of that is, in fact, a humble thing to do, to say that it's not just about us and our time. We are part of a trajectory that has a past and that has a future. Continuity from that past through the present and into the future ties us to all the people who have produced the civilization that we're enjoying in our lifetime.

The precedent that we revere has prepared architects steeped in Classicism for work in a context valuing technological independence. We have a powerful contribution to make, proffering knowledge and experience. Let us do so rationally, accessibly, and with the confidence given us by the institutional sustenance of the Driehaus Prize.

Opposite top:
Rosemary Beach, Florida.
(Photo: Richard Sexton)

Opposite below:
Main Street, Rosemary Beach,
Florida. (Photo: Richard Sexton)

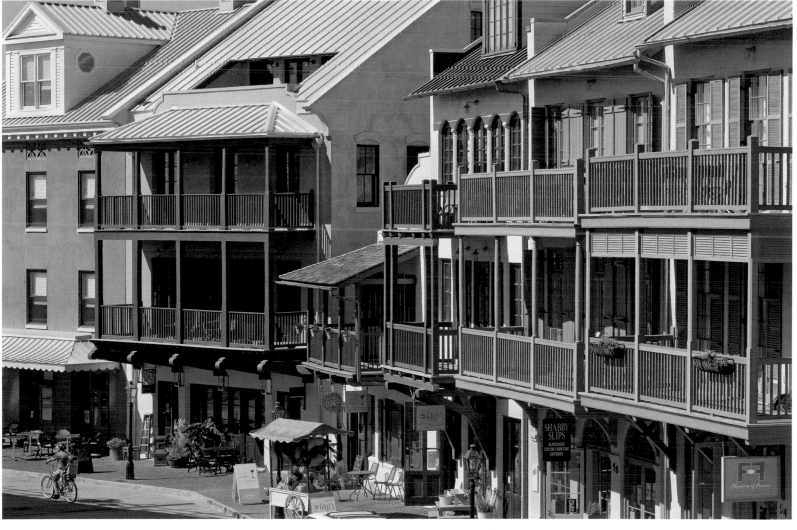

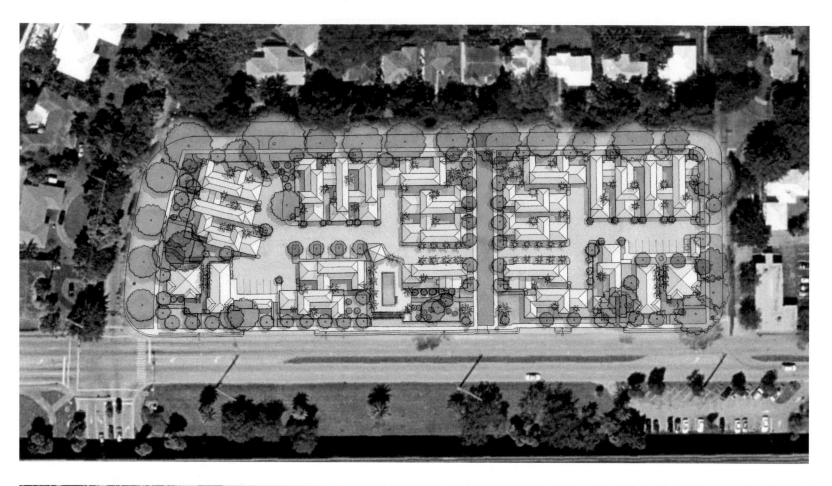

Bermuda Village,
Coral Gables, Florida.
(Photo: Carlos Morales)

Opposite top:
Site plan.

Opposite bottom:
Courtyard homes.

Top right:
Courtyard homes.

Bottom right:
Floor Plans.

Overleaf:
Village of I'On, Mt.
Pleasant, South Carolina.

Rosemary Beach, Walton County, Florida.

Opposite: Alys Beach, Walton County, Florida. (Photo: Tommy Crow)

ABDEL-WAHED
EL-WAKIL

2009 Laureate

Back to Tradition

Our curriculum at the Ain Shams University in Egypt, and all the universities in Egypt, was based on a Beaux-Arts tradition. We spent semesters drawing Corinthian, Doric, and Ionic columns, and our test was to build a three-dimensional plan of an opera house. I found this easy because we lived in one of the prominent examples of Renaissance houses in Egypt.

Then we started doing modern buildings. We were trained to copy from magazines and adopt all the fashions. Architecture became a question of who was the most innovative. Soon after, I was given a post to teach at the university and wondered what I was going to teach. I looked at all the projects that were going up around the Cairo suburbs in 1965, and it was clearly a low point of Modernism. They had taught us the Renaissance style, and then we went into the modern, and we had no idea what Islamic architecture was, or even Egyptian architecture for that matter.

At the time the architectural climate was all about megalomaniac projects—it was the time of President Gamal Abdel Nasser—and in some ways it was like Russia, focusing on state projects, such as nuclear plants and airports. I wanted to know why our contemporary architecture was ugly, especially that which came out of the revolution. The whole of Cairo was populated with four-floor apartment buildings, a staircase, and two flats, like the German worker houses. They sprang up row by row.

About that time a German architect came to Egypt and asked, "Why do you have all this ugly architecture when you have such a beautiful tradition?" He was referring to Islamic architecture, which we were never taught at school. I knew what he was saying—here we were doing a cheap imitation, a parody of German architecture. I began thinking about how I could go back to tradition.

Qubbah Mosque, Medinah, Saudia Arabia.

I didn't have guidance. It was very difficult, because the first pitfall of most of the architecture in Egypt was to merely play with form. We still have people doing this today, building things that appear traditional but do not use traditional methods. It is a devaluation of the form because you lose the relationship of the form with its context.

As I struggled, a friend asked me, "Why don't you go see [Egyptian architect] Hassan Fathy?" Nobody mentioned him in the university, so we didn't know what a treasure he was, a man born around 1900, from the old generation, with a vast knowledge about architecture, philosophy, and life. I think I spent five years with him day and night, the most beautiful years of my life. He was my mentor and completely changed the course of my career.

Fathy reintroduced traditional materials and building techniques, particularly the use of mud brick. He was the author of an acclaimed book, *Architecture for the Poor*, which celebrated the use of local materials.

I believe, as Fathy did, that the solution to many urban problems—pollution, overcrowding, and a homogenous building culture—lies in the countryside, in the undeveloped areas, which are often neglected. The national character of a place remains in the countryside. The village life, the country life, is always abundant, generous, producing. Village life feeds the city; the city is a parasite.

Fathy did nothing for urban planning; he cared about villages. People always asked me, "Why doesn't he do something in Cairo?" And I said, "Because he's looking at the problem at the source." He said, "If I can solve the problem in the country, I would have solved at least 50 percent of the problem in the city, by eliminating migration" to the city. So it's going to the root of the problem to focus on the villages.

For three months he sent me to see all the villages, all the poverty. I saw things that upset my stomach. I saw so much poverty in India and in Egypt, people who were outside the monetary system. This was the beginning of becoming much more aware of living history. Because to a mind trained to think in modern terms, the key idea is that history is finished—*tabula rasa*—and we just start anew. I began to draw different lines between the modernist and the traditionalist, and to examine the Islamic tradition. Through Hassan Fathy, I began to think of architecture as a way of healing the world, as a way of remediating the injustices and improving the lives of people.

Qiblatain Mosque,
Medina, Saudia Arabia.

Island Mosque, Jeddah, Saudia Arabia.

King Saud Mosque, Jeddah, Saudia Arabia.

Halawa House, Agami, Egypt.

Qubbah Mosque, Medinah, Saudia Arabia.

Overleaf:
Miqat Mosque, Jeddah, Saudi Arabia.

Miqat Mosque, Medinah, Saudi Arabia.

Overleaf: Corniche Mosque, Jeddah, Saudi Arabia.

Corniche Mosque,
Jeddah, Saudi Arabia.

Opposite:
Oxford Center for Islamic Studies,
University of Oxford, England.

RAFAEL
MANZANO MARTOS

2010 Laureate

Architectural Toreador

A great bullfighter from Seville, Juan Belmonte, whom I had the honor of knowing, was once criticized by a journalist: "*Maestro*, it is said your style of bullfighting is overly classical." To which Belmonte answered: "Well, if that is what they say about me, it must be true, and I'm very pleased to hear it because, as you know, classical means it never goes out of fashion."

I feel profoundly linked to that great bullfighter, for I too have been greatly criticized for my Classicism, especially among some of my most important colleagues in the profession. One of the few times I received praise for my work was a long time ago from a great architect, the first to be honored with this great award, Léon Krier. I have also received the affection of many clients who have honored me with their confidence and patronage, including the great Director General for Fine Arts in the Spanish Government, Florentino Pérez Embid, and my own *Maestro*, Fernando Chueca, who always supported my architectural efforts.

I had grown accustomed to the criticisms of my work, in which I had sought to perfect the superior classical language of architecture inherited from my professors, in a world that systematically destroys the heritage of its cities, its architecture, and its landscape that I have loved so much.

This language attained its maximum splendor under the two Hispanic Caesars, Trajan and Hadrian, the greatest to govern the Roman world. And at the hand of the great Apollodorus of Damascus and of Hadrian himself, the Architect ruler, who explored in his own villa new architectural ideas that would extend into the latter era of Rome and the early Christian tradition, as well as into the East of Byzantium, Syria and even Islam.

After the fall of the Roman Empire the Western world interpreted the architectural memories of its glorious past and combined them with reflections of Eastern architecture, recreating them

Courtyard of the Maidens, Royal Alcázar, Seville, Spain.

in a style that was both old and new. In the diverse schools of the Gothic and Romanesque period this new architecture emerged is a way that parallels the emergence of the new Anglo-Saxon vernaculars without losing from its vocabulary its ancient roots in classical Greek and Roman.

All this medieval past was in danger of being forgotten because of the profound philological renovation of the ancient language of architecture imposed by Renaissance humanism that, from its birth in the small, yet rich and cultured republics of Italy, was going to sweep across Europe, starting with Spain and France.

The return to that ancient language did not mean a strict replica of the architecture of the classical past but rather the creation of a new architecture that recovered the linguistic perfection of Rome and gave it a new drive and ability to evolve into Mannerism and towards a High Baroque.

Despite its apparent frigidity, Neoclassicism was able to generate a Romantic Classicism, which was continued in the nineteenth century in the historicist evocation of the medieval idioms. All these combined into an eclecticism that was to create one of the largest numbers of buildings and cities ever constructed by humankind. Furthermore, Classicism gave life to Modernism and Art Deco, which in turn would prepare the way to an avant-garde movement based upon a new architecture that was born with the spontaneity of nature. Unfortunately the skyscraper, half a century earlier in Chicago, which was very promising in the hands of an exceptional generation, was not able to develop a new and universal architectural language and today is suffering a crisis.

As in the last moments of the Middle Ages, Classicism is once more a possible option in the search for a new geometry for architecture and a construction technique based on the formal roots and on the local building materials in each region, city, and culture.

I close now with my sincere gratitude. My parents made great sacrifices so that I could achieve my career in architecture. My mother introduced me to the principles of drawing; my siblings first, then my wife, Concha, and my children have accompanied me through the happy and painful days of my life's adventure, filling in for my weaknesses.

I had great teachers in the University of Spain, Torres Balbás, Gómez Moreno and, above all, Fernando Chueca, an architect and the greatest historian of Spanish architecture. And I have had great students, colleagues, and friends, some of them working with me, colleagues at the University and in the academies, full of wisdom in their respective subjects. This prize honours an architecture that is eternally faithful to Classicism, a universal language that has remained valid for the last twenty-five centuries and handed down its colossal architectural and urbanistic heritage to the Western world, a tradition that exceeds in its grandeur the modesty of my merits.

Junction Courtyard, Gothic Palace,
Royal Alcázar, Seville, Spain.

Overleaf:
Mixed-use development,
San Fernando Street,
Seville, Spain.

Previous spread: Courtyard, Hernandez House, Seville, Spain.

Cajasol Building, Plaza de San Francisco, Seville, Spain, street view (Opposite) and main courtyard (Above).

Overleaf: Hallway Cajasol Building.

Living Room, Fajardo House, Pasaje de Andreu Street, Seville, Spain.

Bedroom, Fajardo House, Pasaje de Andreu Street, Seville, Spain.

Hotel Alfonso XIII, Seville, Spain.

Overleaf: Patio de la Monteria, King Don Pedro's Palace, Royal Alcázar, Seville, Spain.

Studio, Fajardo House, Pasaje de Andreu Street, Seville, Spain.

High-Tech Hotel, Munoz y Pabon Street, Seville, Spain.

ROBERT A.M.
STERN

2011 Laureate

Classical and Modern

The Driehaus Prize is the standard bearer for the enduring values of architecture as a continuously evolving discourse rooted in tradition. The great honor of the Driehaus Prize—unquestionably the greatest honor available to those of us who endeavor to pursue a practice of architecture based on age-old principles but also open to new possibilities—means an enormous amount to me personally, and I am hugely flattered to be in the distinguished company of the other esteemed laureates, surely an august group, but especially so as it includes longtime friends and sometime collaborators: Jaquelin Robertson; Allan Greenberg; Léon Krier; Demetri Porphyrios; Quinlan Terry; Abdel-Wahed El-Wakil; Andrés Duany and Elizabeth Plater-Zyberk; and Rafael Manzano Martos. I thank Richard Driehaus for founding an architectural prize unlike any other, one that celebrates design achievement measured by a consistent, time-honored set of principles. Unlike the winners of other architectural prizes who are celebrated for their unique accomplishments, the Driehaus Prize winners are honored for accomplishments realized in relation to shared beliefs.

The Driehaus Prize is a celebration of design research into what is possible and what is desirable, into what an architect can discover about the self, the world, and the art of architecture. The process of design confronts architects with a reality which will be true for them always: that the architecture project is never really finished. The better one gets at architecture, the more one wants to get better still. Architecture is a profession, an art, but most of all, an obsession.

The long trajectory of history has given form to buildings and places that permit men and women to coexist with dignity, to communicate, to share and yet retain a measure of their individuality. Architecture is fundamentally a humanistic discipline. As such, it must be open to the crosscurrents of ideas, welcoming that which is new and challenging while measuring the conflicting

Fifteen Central Park West, New York. (Photo: Peter Aaron/Esto)

Overleaf: Nashville Public Library, Nashville, Tennessee. (Photo: Peter Aaron/Esto)

claims of the present against standards that have prevailed in the past. In a world of competing "isms", of combative certainties, architects do not provide answers so much as ask questions.

I welcome the potential reach of today's global practice, though it is much abused by architects and clients alike, who take it as an opportunity to throw aesthetic caution to the winds of shameless self-promotion. Global practice at its most responsible has the capacity to realize architecture that is neither about a personal signature style nor about abstract, universal, and consequently impersonal modes of expression. Global practice challenges us to bring the advantages of modernity's material benefits to those who need and want them, while not imposing a singular conception of what architecture is or should be. The more we encounter the global, the more we should value the local.

I am as interested in icons as the next architect, I suppose, but I am also interested in the humble buildings that shape the circumstances of daily life. Not every building should knock one's eyes out. There is value in the second glance. For me a sunlit corner in a courtyard or a glimpse of nature in a dense urban setting have within them the ineffable magic of place-making that helps lift lives to higher levels of awareness while dignifying the daily routine. There are many ways of making architecture with many more no doubt to come—the human capacity for invention is limitless—but at the core there are certain standards that always define quality. As architects we need to be ever suspicious of trends masquerading as ideas.

Part of this prize celebrates contributions to architecture through writing. Sometimes, as I consider what I've written over the years, I wish I'd kept my thoughts to myself. As a young architect I wrote to make space for myself, to reach out to members of my own generation and to create intellectual noise that would get the attention of older architects. My early writings were a plea for architecture to be considered as culture, not merely as an enabling discipline. This I still believe is essential to our self-conception as professionals.

As I grew older, I turned more and more to writing about architecture's history, which has been and remains a continual source of pleasure and inspiration. While I enjoy losing myself in a previous period of time, I pick my periods and subjects strategically—New York City, for example, because its success flies in the face of virtually every modernist idea about architecture and urbanism that was drilled into me as a student, most of which I have since come to disdain. Early on I chronicled the career of the Philadelphia architect George Howe, a traditionalist architect who embraced Modernism but came to see its limitations. Howe's example has grounded me these many years. Currently, I am deep into the history of the Anglo-American garden suburb, because it is one of the only viable environmental responses to the challenges of family life in modern times, yet it has been almost completely ignored, in fact even disdained, by the intelligentsia.

These are difficult but interesting times for the profession, as the age-old authority of built form is challenged by the immense imagistic power of electronic media, which some architects find so compelling that they are prepared to overthrow architecture as we know it. Though new times need new solutions, architecture has an obligation to see beyond the moment. It will be too bad if we succumb to the siren song of electronics only to realize that we have traded a physical architecture of solid and void for an illusionistic world of smoke, mirrors, mist, and fog. Architecture must remain true to its own nature and purpose.

The great challenge to the architect is not to have a visionary idea, but to respond to circumstance with something tangible, useful, beautiful, even—something that connects as it challenges. Connects to what and to whom, one may ask. Well, certainly to architecture's own traditions but also to a wide range of people, so that it becomes a part of a common experience. Architecture finds its highest expression when it connects with culture as a whole.

I began to learn how to be an architect at Yale in the early 1960s when, largely because Eero Saarinen had the confidence of Yale's president, A. Whitney Griswold, the university embarked on a major campaign of construction in which some of the most interesting younger architects of the day were encouraged to realize provocative work. It was a privilege to be able to see exciting new buildings being constructed all around the campus. Yet dazzlingly inventive though these new buildings were in and of themselves, with only a few exceptions they made little collective sense.

Two great teachers at Yale, the architect Paul Rudolph, head of the program, and the art historian Vincent Scully, as they each struggled to cast aside the rigid ideological strictures of Modernism, helped open my eyes to a more inclusive view of modern architecture as a whole—one that was grounded in the past and not apart from it as so many then believed. At the deepest level, Rudolph and Scully shared a profound belief that architecture succeeds as it expresses the interrelationship of man, building, and place. Two others joined Scully and Rudolph as significant influences on me. Robert Venturi helped me see the buildings of the past in fresh ways while opening me up to the various ways a modern architect could appropriate them for his or her own purposes in the present. But perhaps most of all, Philip Johnson deeply impressed me with his exhortation: "You cannot not know history."

As a student, I would gaze out the windows of our top-floor studio in Louis Kahn's loft-like art gallery, through which I would contemplate Yale's Gothic skyline of the 1920s and 1930s—widely admired as the physical embodiment of the university by most, except architects, who saw its expressive use of historical precedent as constituent foolishness. I began to wonder about the events that had caused architectural opinion to change so drastically in the twenty or so years between the time when the last of those Gothic Yale buildings had been built and the time when I began my studies. In short, I began to develop doubts about the obsessive present-ness of Modernism.

I am a modern architect but not a modernist. In fact, I am deeply suspicious of isms of any kind and I hope the day will soon come when tradition can be reconciled with modernity, leading to a cessation of the twentieth century's civil war between the two, replacing it with a more nuanced approach that puts human values over ideology and dogma. In hoping for this foolish waste of artistic energy to play to a conclusion, I am encouraged by the words of the great Finnish architect Alvar Aalto, who was frequently asked, "Are you traditional or modern?" To which Aalto would always and wisely reply: "There are only two things in art: humanity and not." Today more than ever architects must be traditional and modern.

The global reach that increasingly characterizes contemporary practice brings with it one certainty: the need for each of us to recognize that there can be no overweening, singular, universally applicable style with which to design our buildings and cities. The modern world is if nothing else

heterogeneous, forcing us to think freely, to keep an open mind, to relish its variety. But an open mind is not to be confused with an unprincipled mind. So I assert that we need the Classical, which is not a style, or merely a repertoire of great buildings, but is a theoretical basis for best practice, a grammar, a syntax, a respect for earth-centered construction—in short a discipline without parallel or peer. For me, the classical tradition is the gateway to the house of architecture. To embrace the classical tradition is to enter into the etymology of architectural form, to release architecture from circumstantial action into realms of meaning rooted in the enduring natural order of the world. The classical tradition is the root, the measure, the datum which gives order to the *lingua franca*, be it derived from traditional craft vernaculars of the pre-industrial past or the mechanical vernaculars of mass production.

In my work as an architect, historian, and educator, I believe one can adhere to classical principles and still be very much a modern architect. This may seem contradictory to some, including some in this room who may see the world of Classicism as inherently combative to that of modernity. But I stand with the early twentieth-century French poet Alain Chartier, who proclaimed, "Nothing is more dangerous than an idea, when you have only one." I believe one can be both Classical and Modern. And I believe, as have many of the notable moderns before me, including Mies van der Rohe, Le Corbusier, and Louis Kahn, that the classical tradition provides true compass points by which architects may guide their individual journeys.

I'd like to say a few words about tradition. There is a profound difference between tradition and custom. Custom is habit. It is fixed. Custom is business as usual, often unthinking, even unconscious. Tradition is deliberate and considered. To value a tradition and to maintain it over time requires a conscious effort and a sense of self. Traditions are very precious—they are talismans, symbols, beliefs. Tradition provides a refuge from the rootlessness of everyday life. But tradition is not fixed. Tradition evolves just as culture evolves. Traditions can be imitated but not initiated. One architect cannot a tradition make.

Architects should stop worrying about self-expression and zeitgeist, which lead to an obsession with saying things *differently* as opposed to saying them *clearly* or *meaningfully*. Obviously each artist dreams of making a contribution, but such contributions are best when made within a context. In embracing tradition, there is no need to throw out invention.

In fact, I believe that without tradition there can be no invention. In 1923, Le Corbusier offered the challenge, "architecture or revolution." For our moment I would propose something different and more conciliatory: tradition *and* modernity.

Architecture is a commitment toward both the discovery of new things and the recovery of valuable things once known and now forgotten. Architecture is invention and affirmation, search and research. It is a vital natural force, an important human activity, a constellation of possibilities; it is the best way humankind has yet devised to shape the world. The hardest thing to do, it seems to me, is to base your work on what is known but then to at once make work that is as good as the model on which it is based and is at the same time fresh and with its own identity. That is the impossible dream for this modern traditional architect—impossible, yes, but a dream still worth dreaming.

Opposite and Overleaf:
Comcast Center,
Philadelphia, Pennsylvania.
(Photos: Peter Aaron)

House at Seaside, Seaside, Florida.
(Photo: Peter Aaron)

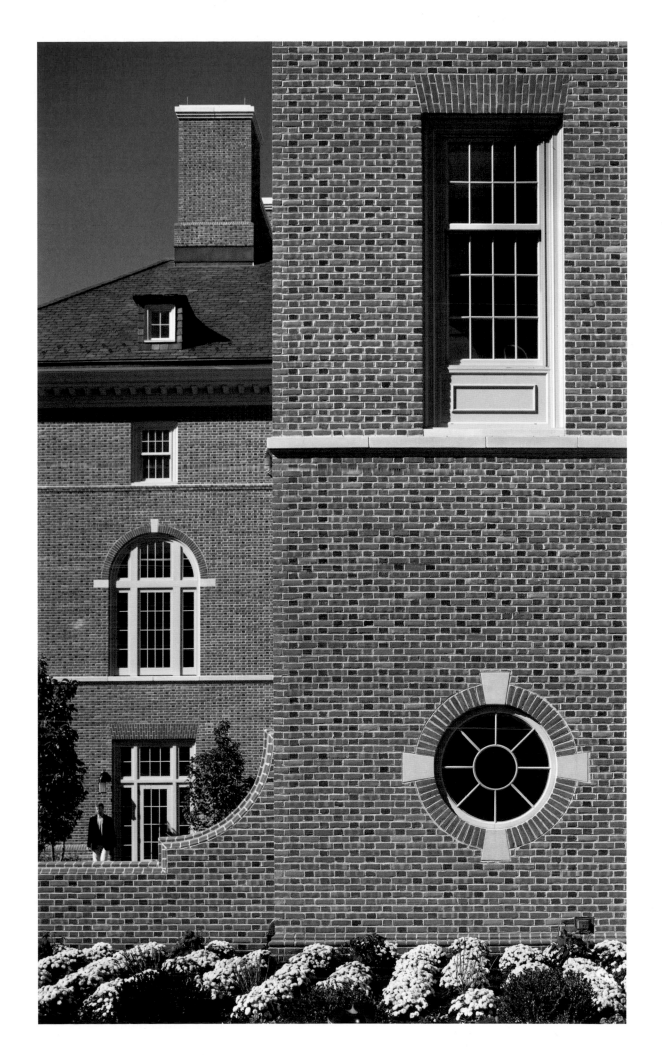

These pages and Overleaf:
Alan B. Miller Hall,
The Mason School of Business,
The College of William and Mary
Williamsburg, Virginia.
(Photo: Peter Aaron)

Fifteen Central Park West,
New York.
(Photo: Peter Aaron)

Overleaf:
Calabasas Civic Centre,
Calabasas, California.
(Photo: Peter Aaron)

MICHAEL
GRAVES

2012 Laureate

Making a Plan

One of the greatest strengths of traditional architecture is its emphasis on the plan. Through shaping rooms and the passages between them, the classical plan influences how we use buildings and how we experience them. This is much harder to achieve in modern architecture because of its fascination with space. When I was in architecture school in the late 1950s, the modernists made it a moral imperative to draw space, not rooms. The bearing wall was anathema and the free plan reigned. I later realized that the modern emphasis on *space* meant the loss of important qualities of the *room*, including fundamental distinctions between, for example, public and private realms. These distinctions create a sense of place and, in a humanistic way, affect how we understand ourselves within the physical world. This became clear to me during the two years that I spent as a Rome Prize Fellow of the American Academy in Rome following graduate school. In Rome, I received an extraordinary visual and cultural education through observing, analyzing, studying, and drawing traditional buildings of all ages.

Just as being in Rome was an experience of a lifetime that shaped my approach to architecture, receiving the Richard H. Driehaus Prize at the University of Notre Dame for me is the honor of a lifetime that acknowledges our common ground. I am touched by Richard's generosity and his passion for the values that traditional architecture can bring to our culture and society. In addition, the time I have spent with Dean Michael Lykoudis and his students at the Notre Dame School of Architecture has been marvelous, as their embrace of the lasting tenets of Classicism outweighs today's all-too-prevalent pursuit of the new. As the tenth recipient of the Driehaus Prize, I am pleased to be in the company of a group of honorees who share Richard's and Michael's vision, and I delight in the conversations and critical debate that we have when we're all together.

During my Driehaus award ceremony in Chicago in March of 2012, I addressed a few remarks to the Notre Dame students in the audience about the importance of the architectural plan. I would like to elaborate on that topic in this short essay for the book commemorating the tenth anniversary of the Driehaus Prize. While I will address only building plans, not landscape or city plans, some of the same lessons apply. In my 39-year teaching career at Princeton University and as a guest critic at other universities, I have frequently analyzed traditional plans with my students

Castalia, Ministry of Health, Welfare and Sport, The Hague, Netherlands.

to advance their understanding of how to make a useful plan. However, I find that very few studio critics address plan-making at all, even though the plan is so crucial to the creation and experience of architecture. For me, architecture school should be a time when our appetites for learning spark a lifelong desire to explore architecture through reading, observation and documentation. And for me that starts with the plan.

As a student in Rome in the early 1960s, I became fascinated not only by the city and its buildings but also by the architectural "literature" about its history. For example, the drawings and etchings of an architect like Piranesi illustrate buildings and ruins in a manner that describes how they were constructed, and how they relate to their surroundings. While seemingly pictorial, his work on closer examination is actually very analytical. Of particular significance to me during the time I spent in Rome was the discovery of the multiple volumes of Paul Letarouilly's *Edifices de Rome Moderne*, published in 1860. These are oversized publications—so-called elephant volumes —of such heft that one can scarcely move them. However, they were also published in a more portable 15 x 10-inch version known as the "student Letarouilly." The volumes on Palaces and Residences and on Convents and Churches meticulously document buildings in Rome through elevations, sections, perspectives, selected details, and of course, through plans. The plans typically depict both the ground floor (the *rez de chaussée*) and *piano nobile* (in Italian), the two "public" levels of the buildings. These plans are rich resources for understanding the proportions and calibration of rooms and the passages between them. Of course, as two-dimensional representations, they are most useful for analytical purposes.

Louwman Museum,
The Hague, Netherlands.
(Photos courtesy
Louwman Museum)

However, the notations of indoors and outdoors as a measure of light, along with the suggestions of ceiling configurations, allow us to imagine what it would be like to traverse the buildings and inhabit the volume of the rooms.

In three dimensions, from the moment that we cross a building's threshold, we are influenced by the plan, and the plan affects our behavior as we move through the building. On that topic, I recall remarks made some years ago by the critic Robert Hughes regarding Beaux Arts planning principles. They struck a chord with me then and still resonate today. He described how the route, or in Beaux Arts parlance the architectural "*marche*," through a building is influenced by slight shifts in the axes that organize the plan. He said that as we are walking, the primary axis of our movement becomes influenced by tendencies that develop to the left or right. In other words, our route shifts based on the inflections of the architecture. For example, let's say that we have entered a building in the center of a façade and are drawn through a vestibule toward a passage straight ahead, the primary axis of movement. After walking for a while, the passage opens onto a rectangular space, half of which aligns with the passage we've been negotiating and the other half expands to the right. This room is thus twice as wide as the passage and inflects our movement toward the right. We will be gently urged to re-center ourselves, and possibly to consider other options for the next leg of our journey depending on secondary or even tertiary axes that become available.

In many traditional plans, the relative sizes and destinations of the passages create a natural hierarchy within the building's circulation, and influence how we center and re-center ourselves. These inflections within the plan, the horizontal organization of the building, are also greatly affected by the section of the building, its vertical organization. For example, if a room has a vault, it will have a linear orientation. If it has a dome, it will be more centralized and the path of movement may not be so clearly defined.

One example of centering and re-centering is Jean Courtonne's 18th century plan of the Hotel de Matignon (now the residence of the French Prime Minister), which I drew in my sketchbook. We enter the complex through an open air courtyard on axis with the main entrance, and our route through the building is re-centered to another axis that leads to a second courtyard and out to the surrounding park. Another more complex example, from Letarouilly, is the plan of the urban church and hospice of Santissima Trinità dei Pellegrini in Rome. Here we see how the church and individual rooms are knit together by a series of passages made legible by the location of courtyards that introduce natural light. Unlike the Maison Domino of Le Corbusier and many modern buildings, with columns that support a flat ceiling slab, traditional buildings illustrated throughout Letarouilly's books have articulated sections.

In the end, while the plan at the ground plane provides the organization of the building, how we navigate and experience it is influenced by the surrounding surfaces, by the forms, articulation and illumination of the walls and ceilings, and in turn by the volumes that they create. Thus the volumetric construct of the plan and the section, as well as the introduction of natural light, the divisions of the walls, the articulation of architectural elements, and the finishes all contribute to the architecture. When you start with "good bones" in the efficacy of the plan, the experience of the place becomes richer and more meaningful.

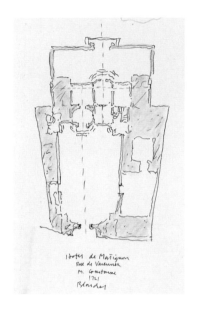

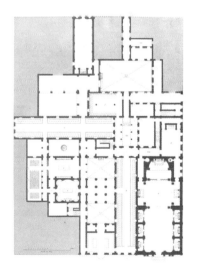

Humana Building, Louisville, Kentucky.

Above top:
Hotel de Matignon, Rue de Varenne, Paris, by Jean Courtonne. Drawing by Michael Graves.

Above bottom:
Parish of Santissima Trinità dei Pellegrini, Rome, Italy, by Letarouilly.

Overleaf:
Denver Public Library, Denver, Colorado.
(Photos: Timothy Hursley)

Hyatt Regency Taba Heights, Taba, Egypt. (Photo: Timothy Hursley)

Garden Grove Restaurant,
Walt Disney World Swan Hotel,
Orlando, Florida.
(Photo: Steven Brooke)

Opposite top:
Team Disney Corporate
Headquarters, Orlando, Florida.
(Photo: Steven Brooke)

Opposite bottom:
Walt Disney World Swan Hotel,
Orlando, Florida.
(Photo: Steven Brooke)

Overleaf:
Miramar Resort Hotel,
El Gouna, Egypt.

Intercontinental Hotel, Taba Heights, Egypt. (Photo courtesy Orascom Touristic Development)

Dining room, El Gouna Golf Hotel, El Gouna, Egypt. (Photo courtesy Orascom Touristic Development)

Overleaf: Martel College, Rice University, Houston, Texas.

Above: Team Disney Corporate Headquarters, Orlando, Florida. (Photo courtesy Orascom Touristic Development)

Opposite: Executive Dining Room, Team Disney Corporate Headquarters, Orlando, Florida.

Key to
A CLASSICAL PERSPECTIVE
the First Decade of the Driehaus Prize

1. Choregic Monument of Lysicrates, Athens
2. Mulberry Guest Lodge, Jaquelin Robertson
3 Skipping Stone, Jaquelin Robertson
4. Casa de Campo Villa, Jaquelin Robertson
5. Plocek House, Michael Graves
6. Graves Residence: The Warehouse, Michael Graves
7. Hibiscus House, Andrés Duany and Elizabeth Plater-Zyberk
8. Mission San Juan Bautista, Andrés Duany and Elizabeth Plater-Zyberk
9. Hay Barn, Jaquelin Robertson
10. Westover House, Andrés Duany and Elizabeth Plater-Zyberk
11. Sheftall House, Andrés Duany and Elizabeth Plater-Zyberk

12. Krier House, Seaside, Léon Krier
13. Vilanova House, Andrés Duany and Elizabeth Plater-Zyberk
14. House at Seaside, Robert A.M. Stern
15. Abrage Mosque, Abdel-Wahed El-Wakil
16. Halawa House, Abdel-Wahed El-Wakil
17. Pyramid House, Abdel-Wahed El-Wakil
18. House in Hydra, Abdel-Wahed El-Wakil
19. Lake Pavilion, Watercolor, Jaquelin Robertson
20. Belvedere Village, Demetri Porphyrios
21. Corinthian Villa, Regents Park, Quinlan Terry
22. Nymphaeum, West Green, Quinlan Terry
23. Maitland Robinson Library, Cambridge, Quinlan Terry

24. Grove Quarangle, Magdalen College, Oxford, Demetri Porphyrios
25. Richmond Riverside, Quinlan Terry
26. County of Charleston Judicial Center, Jaquelin Robertson
27. New Albany Country Club, Jaquelin Robertson
28. Seaside Tower, Léon Krier
29. Clos Pegase Winery, Michael Graves
30. Whitman College, Princeton University, Demetri Porphyrios
31. Denver Central Library, Michael Graves
32. Portland Building, Michael Graves
33. Humana Building, Michael Graves
34. Three Brindley Place, Demetri Porphyrios

35. Kasumi Research and Training Center, Michael Graves
36. Edgewater Apartments, Vancouver, Robert A.M. Stern
37. Fargo-Moorhead Cultural Center, Michael Graves
38. Jeddah Lighthouse, Abdel-Wahed El-Wakil
39. Alys Beach Townhouse, Andrés Duany and
    Elizabeth Plater-Zyberk
40. Calle San Fernando, Sevilla, Rafael Manzano Martos
41. Lewis Gintner Botanical Garden, Jaquelin Robertson
42. Plaza de San Francisco, Sevilla, Rafael Manzano Martos
43. Duncan Galleries, Demetri Porphyrios
44. Corniche Mosque, Abdel-Wahed El-Wakil
45. Real Alcázar de Sevilla, Rafael Manzano Martos

46. Casa Chueca, Sevilla, Rafael Manzano Martos
47. Miqat Mosque, Abdel-Wahed El-Wakil
48. Crown American Building, Michael Graves
49. Church of the Immaculate Conception, Allan Greenberg
50. Colgate Darden School of Business Administration,
    Robert A.M. Stern
51. House of Worship, Tehran, Quinlan Terry
52. Spring Valley Residence, Allan Greenberg
53. Humanities Building, Rice University, Allan Greenberg
54. Gore Hall, University of Delaware, Allan Greenberg
55. McGlothlin Street Hall, College of William and Mary,
    Allan Greenberg

56. Ohrstrom Library, St. Paul's School, Robert A.M. Stern
57. Temple of Venus, West Wycombe, Quinlan Terry
58. Residence in Starwood, Robert A.M. Stern
59. Palo Alto Residence, Robert A.M. Stern
60. Residence, Hewlett Harbour, Robert A.M. Stern
61. Residence in Montecito, Robert A.M. Stern
62. Town of Pitiousa, Demetri Porphyrios
63. Residence in Los Angeles, Robert A.M. Stern
64. Atlantis, Léon Krier

LAUREATE
BIOGRAPHIES

Léon Krier

2003

As a leader of the intellectual framework of the New Traditional and the New Urbanist Movements, Léon Krier is best known as the architect of The Prince of Wales's model town of Poundbury in Dorset, England. Krier taught architecture and town planning at the Royal College of Art, London; Princeton University; the University of Virginia; Yale University, and the University of Notre Dame. He is a founding trustee of the New School for Traditional Architecture & Urbanism in Charleston, South Carolina. Krier's honors include the Jefferson Memorial Gold Medal; the Berlin Prize for Architecture; the Chicago American Institute of Architects Award; the European Culture Prize; and the inaugural Richard H. Driehaus Prize at the University of Notre Dame. The author of several books, Krier's *Architecture: Choice or Fate* was awarded the Silver Medal of the Académie Française. A native Luxembourger who lived in London for 20 years, Krier makes his home in the south of France and Madrid.

Demetri Porphyrios
2004

Dr. Demetri Porphyrios is the principal of the London-based Porphyrios Associates. Porphyrios's lifelong commitment to traditional and classical architecture includes buildings and urban projects in Europe, the United States and the Middle East. He designed the Grove Quadrangle at Magdalen College, Oxford University, and Princeton University's Whitman College. Other well-known projects include the Belvedere Village in Ascot, England; the town of Pitiousa in Spetses, Greece; the Battery Park City pavilion in New York; the Duncan Galleries, Lincoln, Nebraska; the Brindleyplace office buildings in Birmingham, England; and the King's Cross master plan in London. Porphyrios was educated at Princeton University where he received his master of architecture and his PhD in the history and theory of architecture. Porphyrios's books include *Sources of Modern Eclecticism*, *On the Methodology of Architectural History*, *Classicism is not a Style*, *Building and Rational Architecture*, and *Classical Architecture*.

Quinlan Terry

2005

Quinlan Terry is principal of Quinlan and Francis Terry Architects. Terry's work includes the redesign of three State rooms at 10 Downing Street, the historic office and home of the British Prime Minister; Merchant Square at Colonial Williamsburg; and the Richmond Riverside Development in Surrey, England, a large development with offices, apartments, restaurants, and community gardens which has become an icon of traditional urban design. Other projects include a series of villas in Regents Park, London; an office block in Paternoster Square next to St. Paul's Cathedral in London; and the new Brentwood Cathedral in Essex, England. Educated at London's Architectural Association, Terry was also a Rome Scholar sponsored by The British School at Rome, which promotes education in architecture, fine art, and history. In 1984 he received the European Architecture Prize Philippe Rotthier and in 2002 he was honored with an Arthur Ross Award from the Institute of Classical Architecture and Art.

Allan Greenberg

2006

The first American architect to receive the Driehaus Prize, Allan Greenberg is "the most knowing, most serious practitioner of Classicism currently on the scene in this country," says George Hersey, author and professor of Art History at Yale University. Greenberg's State Department renovation restored the grandeur the Founding Fathers envisioned. Other celebrated works include the Humanities Building at Rice University, which won the American Institute of Architects 2001 Design Excellence Award from the Washington, D.C. chapter. Greenberg designed the Brooks Brothers Store in Beverly Hills, named the Best Commercial Building of 1998 by the Precast/Prestressed Concrete Institute. A Greenwich, Connecticut farmhouse won a 1990 Arthur Ross Award from Classical America for outstanding architectural rendering. Greenberg's books include *Lutyens and the Modern Movement*, *The Architecture of Democracy: The Founding Fathers' Vision for America* and *George Washington, Architect*.

Jaquelin Robertson

2007

Jaquelin Robertson is a partner in the firm Cooper, Robertson & Partners and founder of the New York City Urban Design Group. He served under John Lindsay as the Director of the Mayor's Office of Midtown Planning and Development and worked as a New York City Planning Commissioner. Committed to introducing "human values into urban plans," he founded the Jeffersonian Restoration Advisory Board and the Mayor's Institute on City Design. He has been a consultant to the Ford Foundation, the Government of Jamaica, the Federal Highway Administration, and the National Capital Development Commission in Canberra, Australia. In 1975, Robertson directed the design of Iran's new capital center, Shahestan Pahlavi. Robertson has received numerous design awards, including the 1998 Thomas Jefferson Foundation Medal in Architecture and the 2002 Seaside Prize for his contributions to American urbanism. A Richmond, Virginia native, Robertson received his B.A. and M.Arch from Yale University and was a Rhodes Scholar at Magdalen College, Oxford.

Andrés Duany and Elizabeth Plater-Zyberk

2008

Andrés Duany and Elizabeth Plater-Zyberk, the husband and wife team who lead the Miami firm Duany Plater-Zyberk & Company (DPZ), are two of the most influential architects and town planners in the country. Best known for designing cities—street grids, town centers, parks—and for writing architectural and building codes that help revitalize communities, their firm has completed designs for nearly 300 new towns, regional plans, and revitalization projects, including neighborhoods in Naples, Fla., Baton Rouge, La. and Providence, R.I. Plater-Zyberk, the dean of Miami School of Architecture, also leads Miami 21, a project to overhaul city zoning. Duany and Plater-Zyberk have received numerous design awards, including the Brandeis Award for Architecture, the Thomas Jefferson Memorial Medal of Architecture, the Vincent J. Scully Prize for exemplary practice and scholarship in architecture and urban design from the National Building Museum, and the Seaside Prize for contributions to community planning and design from The Seaside Institute. Duany and Plater-Zyberk met as undergraduates at Princeton University and both received master's degrees from the Yale School of Architecture.

Abdel-Wahed El-Wakil

2009

Abdel-Wahed El-Wakil is one of the leading voices in contemporary Islamic architecture and a practitioner known worldwide for his use of traditional form and technique. Over the past four decades, El-Wakil has built mosques, public buildings, and private residences throughout the Middle East. His work—which includes the Halawa House in Agamy, Egypt, for which he won his first Aga Khan Award for Architecture; the residence of Ahmed Sulaiman in Jeddah; and the new Quba Mosque in Medina— uses traditional design principles with indigenous materials and processes. El-Wakil is also well known for the King Saud Mosque in Jeddah, Saudi Arabia and the Oxford University Centre for Islamic Studies, designed at the request of The Prince of Wales.

Rafael Manzano Martos

2010

Rafael Manzano Martos is a Spanish architect known for his distinctive use of the Mudéjar style. Mudéjar emerged as a style blending Muslim and Christian influences in the 12th century on the Iberian Peninsula. With expertise in this style and a command of the Western and Islamic vernaculars, Manzano has designed hotels and other commercial buildings, along with homes and residential complexes throughout Spain and the Middle East. His best-known work includes homes for the architect Fernando Chueca Goitia in Seville and the bullfighter Curro Romero in Marbella (now a Julio Iglesias property). His fluency in Islamic style is evident in his designs for a hotel in Mosul, Iraq, and a hotel resort and shopping district in Riyadh, Saudi Arabia. Manzano, professor emeritus at the Seville Superior Technical School of Architecture, received his PhD from the Architecture School of Madrid. His career has included building restoration, urban planning, and teaching, in addition to his architectural work. Manzano served as the Director-Curator and Governor of the Alcázar of Seville.

Robert A. M. Stern

2011

Robert A. M. Stern, whose influential designs revitalized traditional architecture, is founder and senior partner of Robert A. M. Stern Architects and Dean of the Yale School of Architecture. Stern's work as an architect is rooted in the principles, values, and ideals of Classicism and traditional architecture. Comcast Center, a prismatic glass curtainwall office tower in Philadelphia carries forward the proportions of the classical obelisk; the acclaimed residential tower 15 Central Park West recaptures the spirit of New York's great pre-war apartment houses; the influential plan for Celebration, Florida, is grounded in a decades-long study of traditional town planning. His current projects include the design of the George W. Bush Presidential Center at Southern Methodist University in Dallas, Texas, and two new residential colleges in the Gothic mode at Yale.

Michael Graves

2012

Michael Graves is founding principal of the firm Michael Graves & Associates (MGA) and the Robert Schirmer Professor of Architecture, Emeritus at Princeton University, where he taught for 39 years. At Princeton, Graves reintroduced the principles of traditional and classical composition and also brought a dedication to urbanism to a modernist curriculum. Receiving the Rome Prize in 1960 as a scholar at the American Academy in Rome, where he is now a Trustee, Graves was influenced by "the timeless grammar" of architecture that he has applied to his own work. In structures such as the Portland (Oregon) Public Services Building and Humana Corporation headquarters in Louisville, Kentucky, Graves's designs are characterized for their attention to detail and dignity. His influential designs extend from buildings including the iconic Denver Central Library to everyday objects such as his celebrated Alessi kettle. The beauty and quality of ordinary objects, Graves believes, have the power to affect the soul.

THE JURY

A panel of distinguished jurors selects a leading traditional and classical architect to receive The Richard H. Driehaus Prize at the University of Notre Dame. The jury also honors another individual with the Henry Hope Reed Award for notable contributions to the promotion and preservation of classical art and architecture. Jury meetings are held in a city of great architectural significance—including Paris, London, Prague, Buenos Aires, New York, and Washington, D.C., during the Driehaus Prize's first decade—settings where the urban fabric becomes an inspirational backdrop for deliberations.

The Driehaus Prize thanks those who have served on the jury: Thomas H. Beeby, Adele Chatfield-Taylor, Robert Davis, Elizabeth Meredith Dowling, Anne Fairfax, Thomas Fisher, Paul Goldberger, Léon Krier, Elizabeth Plater-Zyberk, Jaquelin Robertson, Witold Rybczynski, David M. Schwarz, and David Watkin.

THE RICHARD H. DRIEHAUS PRIZE
AT THE UNIVERSITY OF NOTRE DAME

INDEX

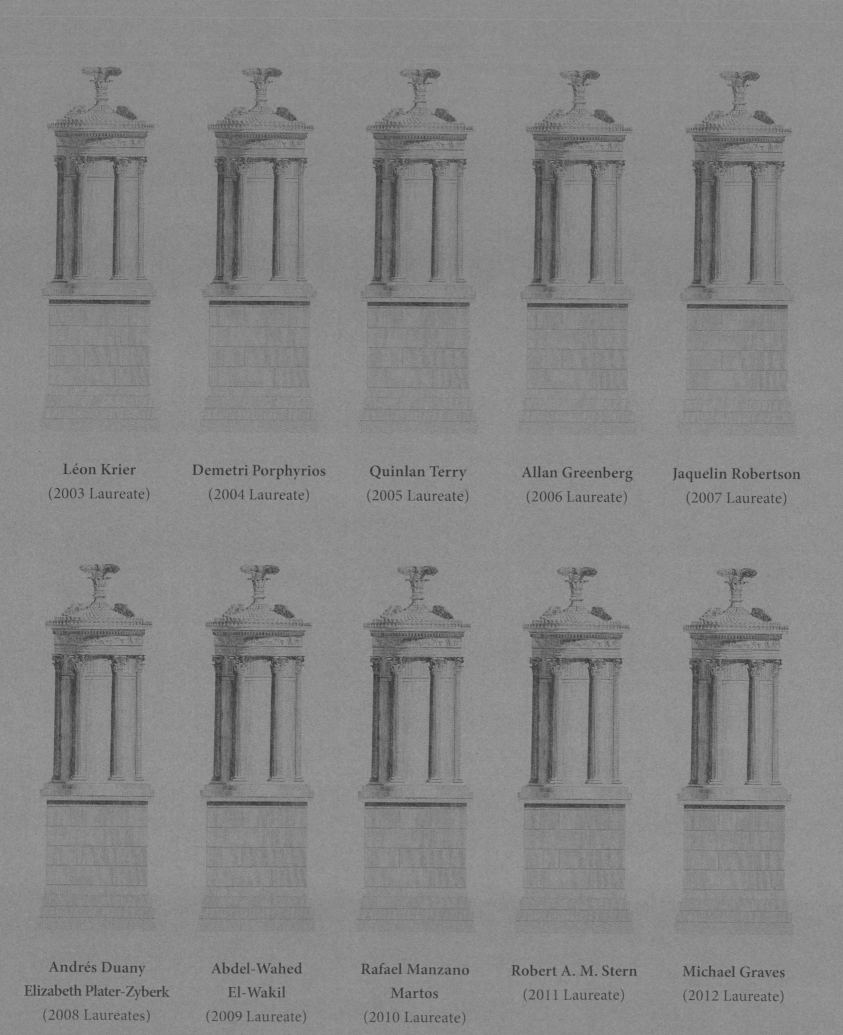

Léon Krier
(2003 Laureate)

Demetri Porphyrios
(2004 Laureate)

Quinlan Terry
(2005 Laureate)

Allan Greenberg
(2006 Laureate)

Jaquelin Robertson
(2007 Laureate)

Andrés Duany
Elizabeth Plater-Zyberk
(2008 Laureates)

Abdel-Wahed
El-Wakil
(2009 Laureate)

Rafael Manzano
Martos
(2010 Laureate)

Robert A. M. Stern
(2011 Laureate)

Michael Graves
(2012 Laureate)